FREMDSPRACHENTEXTE

English Love Poems

Ausgewählt und herausgegeben
von Eva-Maria König

Philipp Reclam jun. Stuttgart

Umschlagabbildung: Dante Gabriel Rossetti, Titelzeichnung zu: Christina Rossetti, *Goblin Market and Other Poems* (1862)

RECLAMS UNIVERSAL-BIBLIOTHEK Nr. 9283

Aktualisierte Ausgabe 2010
Gesamtherstellung: Reclam, Ditzingen. Printed in Germany 2010

ISBN 978-3-15-009283-5

www.reclam.de

Vorbemerkung

»It was a lover and his lass« – eine alle Liebeslyrik inspirierende Grundkonstellation oder eine im Arkadisch-Märchenhaften angesiedelte Beziehungsvorstellung, die allenfalls im Volkslied überlebt, ansonsten aber durch Reduzierung und Trivialisierung so banal erscheint, daß sie mit lyrischer Kunst kaum noch zu tun haben kann?
Zweifellos hat Liebeslyrik wie alles menschliche Sprechen eine historische Dimension, wenn auch ihr Gegenstand universalen Charakter hat. Die große Bedeutung der Liebe als Thema von Dichtung und die Vielzahl der Liebesgedichte zeigt hier wie bei kaum einem anderen Thema, daß jeder neue Ansatz sich einer Traditionsfülle gegenübersieht, die ihn zu einer künstlerischen Gratwanderung zwischen Wiederholung des schon längst Gesagten und zwanghafter Originalität werden läßt. Dieses Wissen um die Übermacht der Tradition prägt gerade die moderne Liebeslyrik, die häufig die Gefahr des klischeehaften Sprechens von Liebe oder aber die Quellen, aus denen sie schöpft, selbst thematisiert.
Die vorliegende Anthologie soll mit ihrer chronologischen Anordnung einen kleinen Einblick in Liebeslyrik als historischen Prozeß vermitteln. Sie setzt im 16. Jahrhundert ein, zu einem Zeitpunkt, als sich neben der volkstümlichen Dichtung die Traditionsstränge der Minnelieder der provenzalischen Troubadours und der Lyrik der italienischen Renaissance auf englischem Boden bereits zu hohem Rang entwickelt hatten und als »courtly love poetry« ein festes Repertoire an Formen und Ausdrucksmöglichkeiten umfaßten, zu denen insbesondere das Sonett gehörte. Die Lyrik Sir Philip Sidneys, eines Hauptvertreters des englischen Petrarkismus, zeigt, wie hier bereits die klassisch gewordene Form und die allegorisierende Bildlichkeit subtil genutzt werden, um individuelles Empfinden darzustellen.

Dichtung als Prozeß heißt neben der Auseinandersetzung mit der Dichtungstradition auch Dichtung im jeweils verschiedenen historischen Kontext, wobei geschichtliche Realität wie auch geistesgeschichtliche Strömungen und die mit ihnen einhergehenden veränderten Auffassungen von Liebe ihren Niederschlag finden. Das höfische Leben zur Zeit Elisabeths I. und ihres Nachfolgers Jakob I. begünstigte die Dichtung, namentlich die Liebeslyrik; die kühne intellektuelle Bildlichkeit der »metaphysical poets«, als deren Vertreter hier Donne steht, findet eine Entsprechung in einer Zeit, die nicht nur geographisch ihre Grenzen erweiterte, sondern deren gesamtes Weltbild durch die kopernikanische Wende neu strukturiert wurde. Der englische Bürgerkrieg und das Regime der Puritaner setzten dieser Zeit ein jähes Ende und entzogen der Liebeslyrik ihren Nährboden. Das Bestreben, nach der Restauration der Stuarts wieder an die höfische Tradition anzuknüpfen, wurde gefördert durch den sinnenfrohen Karl II., der aus dem französischen Exil galanten Rokokogeschmack mitbrachte. Die neue Dichtung war geistreich, frivol und antipuritanisch, sie blieb in ihrer Bedeutung aber begrenzt. Eine wirklich neue große Zeit der Lyrik brach erst wieder jenseits von höfischer Eleganz mit der Romantik an. Doch wenn auch die Romantik Dichtung mit Wordsworths berühmtem Wort als »emotion recollected in tranquillity« verstand, so war diese Emotion selten Liebe, sondern galt dem Verhältnis des Dichters zur sichtbaren Natur als Symbol einer unsichtbaren bedeutenderen Wirklichkeit. Die großen englischen Romantiker haben alle Liebeslyrik geschrieben, doch sind dies nicht die Gedichte, auf denen ihr Ruhm gründet. Im späten 19. Jahrhundert entwickelte sich in der Liebeslyrik eine neue thematische Perspektive, die bis in die Gegenwart wirksam ist und die auf einem Grundton der Bitterkeit und Skepsis beruht. Immer schon war der schmachtende, melancholische, verschmähte, betrogene Liebhaber Teil der Liebesdichtung gewesen, mit der tieferen psychologischen Einsicht in die Komplexität des menschlichen Charakters erhoben sich jetzt aber Zweifel an der Möglichkeit absoluter menschlicher Liebe. Damit trat das Thema des Sieges der Liebe über die Zeit, eines der zentralen Themen des 16. und 17. Jahrhunderts, endgültig zurück und wich einem Ringen um ein Dennoch angesichts einer als der Liebe feindlich gegenüberstehend empfundenen psychologischen wie auch gesellschaftlichen Situation. Damit rückte auch die Alltagsrealität stärker ins Blickfeld. Die Liebe als den Menschen auszeichnende Fähigkeit ist Teil des menschlichen Selbstbewußtseins, als individuelle Erfahrung ist sie so vielfältig wie das Leben der Menschen selbst. Auch diesem Umstand versucht die vorliegende Anthologie Rechnung zu tragen, indem verschiedene Aspekte von Liebe nicht nur im Hinblick auf historische Entwicklung, sondern auch auf synchroner Ebene ausgewählt wurden, wobei ein Schwerpunkt hier auf dem 20. Jahrhundert liegt. Blakes und Clares Gedichte entfernen sich dabei am weitesten von der Grundkonstellation zweier liebender Menschen, indem sie Liebe als soziale Qualität beziehungsweise als Grundprinzip der belebten Natur betrachten. Das Spektrum der englischen Liebeslyrik, von dem hier nur ein kleiner Ausschnitt vorgestellt werden kann, mag beitragen zur Erörterung dessen, was Philip Larkin nicht als Wahrheit, sondern eher als Frage formuliert: »What will survive of us is love«.

Eva-Maria König

With how sad steps, ô Moone, thou climb'st the skies,
  How silently, and with how wanne a face,
  What, may it be that even in heav'nly place
That busie archer his sharpe arrowes tries?
Sure, if that long with *Love* acquainted eyes
  Can judge of *Love*, thou feel'st a Lover's case;
  I reade it in thy lookes, thy languisht grace,
To me that feele the like, thy state descries.
  Then ev'n of fellowship, ô Moone, tell me
Is constant *Love* deem'd there but want of wit?
Are Beauties there as proud as here they be?
Do they above love to be lov'd, and yet
  Those Lovers scorne whom that *Love* doth possesse?
  Do they call *Vertue* there ungratefulnesse?

(*Astrophel and Stella* XXXI)

2 **wanne:** *wan:* bleich, fahl. – 4 **archer:** Bogenschütze. – 7 **languisht:** *languished:* ermattet, siech, schmachtend. – 8 **to descry:** entdecken, enthüllen, erkennen lassen. – 9 **ev'n:** hier: gleich. – 14 **vertue:** *virtue.*

Let me not to the marriage of true minds
Admit impediments. Love is not love
Which alters when it alteration finds,
Or bends with the remover to remove.
O no, it is an ever-fixed mark
That looks on tempests and is never shaken;
It is the star to every wand'ring bark,
Whose worth's unknown, although his height be taken.
Love's not time's fool, though rosy lips and cheeks
Within his bending sickle's compass come.
Love alters not with his brief hours and weeks,
But bears it out ev'n to the edge of doom.
If this be error and upon me proved,
I never writ, nor no man ever loved.

(*Sonnets* CXVI)

2 **impediment:** Hindernis. – 7 **bark:** Barke, Boot. – 10 **sickle:** Sichel. – **compass:** Bereich, Umkreis. – 12 **doom:** Untergang; Jüngstes Gericht. – 14 **writ** (obs.): *wrote*.

JOHN DONNE

The Good-morrow

I wonder by my troth, what thou, and I
  Did, till we lov'd? were we not wean'd till then?
But suck'd on countrey pleasures, childishly?
  Or snorted we i'the seaven sleepers den?
'Twas so; But this, all pleasures fancies bee.
If ever any beauty I did see,
Which I desir'd, and got, 'twas but a dreame of thee.

And now good morrow to our waking soules,
  Which watch not one another out of feare;
For love, all love of other sights controules,
  And makes one little roome, an every where.
Let sea-discoverers to new worlds have gone,
Let Maps to others, worlds on worlds have showne,
Let us possesse our world, each hath one, and is one.

My face in thine eye, thine in mine appeares,
  And true plaine hearts doe in the faces rest,
Where can we finde two better hemispheares
  Without sharpe North, without declining West?
What ever dyes, was not mixt equally;
If our two loves be one, or, thou and I
Love so alike, that none doe slacken, none can die.

[Titel] **good-morrow** (obs.): guten Morgen!; Morgengruß. – 1 **by my troth:** wahrlich, auf mein Wort (*troth:* Treue, Wahrheit). – 2 **wean'd:** entwöhnt. – 4 **to snort:** 1. (obs.) schnarchen; 2. schnaufen. – **the seven sleepers:** die Siebenschläfer (nach der Legende sieben christliche Brüder, die bei der Verfolgung unter Decius in eine Höhle bei Ephesus flüchteten, dort eingemauert wurden und zweihundert Jahre lang schliefen). – **den:** Höhle, Grube. – 17 **hemispheare:** *hemisphere:* Hemisphäre, Halbkugel – 21 **to slacken:** erschlaffen, nachlassen.

To his Coy Mistress

Had we but World enough, and Time,
This coyness Lady were no crime.
We would sit down, and think which way
To walk, and pass our long Loves Day.
Thou by the *Indian Ganges* side
Should'st Rubies find: I by the Tide
Of *Humber* would complain. I would
Love you ten years before the Flood:
And you should if you please refuse
Till the Conversion of the *Jews*.
My vegetable Love should grow
Vaster then Empires, and more slow.
An hundred years should go to praise
Thine Eyes, and on thy Forehead Gaze.
Two hundred to adore each Breast:
But thirty thousand to the rest.
An Age at least to every part,
And the last Age should show your Heart.
For Lady you deserve this State;
Nor would I love at lower rate.
  But at my back I alwaies hear
Times winged Charriot hurrying near:
And yonder all before us lye
Desarts of vast Eternity.

[Titel] **coy:** zurückhaltend, spröde, sittsam. – 6 **ruby:** Rubin. – 7 **Humber:** Flußmündung an der englischen Ostküste. – 8 **the Flood:** die Sintflut. – 10 **conversion:** Bekehrung. – **Jew:** Jude. – 11 **vegetable:** pflanzlich, mit Lebens- und Wachstumsfähigkeit ausgestattet. – 22 **charriot:** *chariot:* (Streit-, Triumph-)Wagen. – 23 **yonder:** dort drüben.

Thy Beauty shall no more be found;
Nor, in thy marble Vault, shall sound
My ecchoing Song: then Worms shall try
That long preserv'd Virginity:
And your quaint Honour turn to dust;
And into ashes all my Lust.
The Grave's a fine and private place,
But none I think do there embrace.
Now therefore, while the youthful hew
Sits on thy skin like morning dew,
And while thy willing Soul transpires
At every pore with instant Fires,
Now let us sport us while we may;
And now, like am'rous birds of prey,
Rather at once our Time devour,
Than languish in his slow-chapt pow'r.
Let us roll all our Strength, and all
Our sweetness, up into one Ball:
And tear our Pleasures with rough strife,
Thorough the Iron gates of Life.
Thus, though we cannot make our Sun
Stand still, yet we will make him run.

26 **vault:** Gewölbe, Gruft. – 29 **quaint:** wunderlich, altmodisch; stolz; geziert. – 30 **lust:** (Sinnen-)Lust. – 33 **hew:** *hue:* Farbe, Färbung. – 35 **to transpire:** ausdünsten. – 36 **instant:** gegenwärtig, dringend, drängend. – 37 **to sport o.s.:** sich vergnügen, amüsieren, der Liebe frönen. – 38 **am'rous:** *amorous:* verliebt. – 39 **to devour:** verschlingen. – 40 **to languish:** schmachten. – **slow-chapt:** langsam kauend (*chap:* Maul, Kinnbacken). – 43 **strife:** Streit, Kampf, Bemühen, Gewalt. – 44 **thorough:** *through*.

WILLIAM BLAKE

The Clod & the Pebble

"Love seeketh not Itself to please,
Nor for itself hath any care,
But for another gives its ease,
And builds a Heaven in Hell's despair."

So sang a little Clod of Clay
Trodden with the cattle's feet,
But a Pebble of the brook
Warbled out these metres meet:

"Love seeketh only Self to please,
To bind another to Its delight,
Joys in another's loss of ease,
And builds a Hell in Heaven's despite."

(Songs of Experience)

[Titel] **clod:** (Lehm-, Erd-)Klumpen. – **pebble:** Kieselstein. – 8 **to warble:** trillern, schmettern. – **metre:** Versmaß; hier: Vers. – **meet:** passend, geeignet. – 11 **to joy in s.th.:** sich an etwas erfreuen. – 12 **in despite:** zum Trotz.

A Red Red Rose

O my Luve's like a red, red rose,
  That's newly sprung in June;
O my Luve's like the melodie
  That's sweetly play'd in tune. –

As fair art thou, my bonie lass,
  So deep in luve am I;
And I will love thee still, my Dear,
  Till a' the seas gang dry. –

Till a' the seas gang dry, my Dear,
  And the rocks melt wi' the sun:
I will love thee still, my Dear,
  While the sands o' life shall run. –

And fare thee weel, my only Luve!
  And fare thee weel, a while!
And I will come again, my Luve,
  Tho' it were ten thousand mile! –

1 **luve:** *love.* – 5 **art:** *are.* – **bonie:** *bonny*: hübsch, munter. – **lass:** Mädchen. – 8 **a':** *all.* – **gang:** *go.* – 13 **weel:** *well.* – 16 **tho':** *though.*

Strange fits of passion have I known:
And I will dare to tell,
But in the Lover's ear alone,
What once to me befell.

When she I loved looked every day
Fresh as a rose in June,
I to her cottage bent my way,
Beneath an evening-moon.

Upon the moon I fixed my eye,
All over the wide lea;
With quickening pace my horse drew nigh
Those paths so dear to me.

And now we reached the orchard-plot;
And, as we climbed the hill,
The sinking moon to Lucy's cot
Came near, and nearer still.

In one of those sweet dreams I slept,
Kind Nature's gentlest boon!
And all the while my eyes I kept
On the descending moon.

My horse moved on; hoof after hoof
He raised, and never stopped:
When down behind the cottage roof,
At once, the bright moon dropped.

1 **fit:** Anfall, Anwandlung. – 4 **to befall s.o.:** jdm. widerfahren, zustoßen. – 10 **lea:** Flur, Aue. – 11 **to draw nigh:** sich nähern. – 13 **orchard-plot:** Obstgarten, Teil des Gartens mit Obstbäumen. – 15 **Lucy:** s. S. 76. – **cot:** Hütte, Häuschen. – 18 **boon:** Wohltat.

What fond and wayward thoughts will slide
Into a Lover's head!
"O mercy!" to myself I cried,
"If Lucy should be dead!"

(*Poems Founded on the Affections* VII)

25 **wayward:** launenhaft, eigensinnig, unberechenbar.

When we two parted
   In silence and tears,
Half broken-hearted
   To sever for years,
Pale grew thy cheek and cold,
   Colder thy kiss;
Truly that hour foretold
   Sorrow to this.

The dew of the morning
   Sunk chill on my brow –
It felt like the warning
   Of what I feel now.
Thy vows are all broken,
   And light is thy fame;
I hear thy name spoken,
   And share in its shame.

They name thee before me,
   A knell to mine ear;
A shudder comes o'er me –
   Why wert thou so dear?
They know not I knew thee,
   Who knew thee too well: –
Long, long shall I rue thee,
   Too deeply to tell.

In secret we met –
   In silence I grieve,
That thy heart could forget,
   Thy spirit deceive.

4 **to sever:** sich trennen. – 18 **knell:** Totenglocke. – 20 **wert:** *were*. – 23 **to rue:** beklagen, bedauern.

If I should meet thee
After long years,
How should I greet thee! –
With silence and tears.

A Spring Morning

The Spring comes in with all her hues and smells,
In freshness breathing over hills and dells,
O'er woods where May her gorgeous drapery flings,
And meads washed fragrant by their laughing springs.
Fresh are new-opened flowers, untouched and free
From the bold rifling of the amorous bee.
The happy time of singing birds is come,
And love's lone pilgrimage now finds a home;
Among the mossy oaks now coos the dove,
And the hoarse crow finds softer notes for love.
The foxes play around their dens and bark
In joy's excess, mid woodland shadows dark.
The flowers join lips below, the leaves above,
And every sound that meets the ear is love.

1 **hue:** Farbe, Färbung. – 2 **dell:** Tal, Schlucht. – 3 **drapery:** (drapiertes) Tuch, Faltenwurf. – 4 **mead** (poet.): *meadow*. – **spring:** Quelle. – 6 **rifling:** Raub, Plünderung. – **amorous:** verliebt. – 8 **lone:** (poet.) *lonely*. – **pilgrimage:** Pilgerfahrt, Wallfahrt. – 9 **to coo:** gurren. – 10 **hoarse:** heiser. – 11 **den:** Höhle, Grube. – 12 **mid** (poet.): *amid*.

Bright star! would I were steadfast as thou art –
Not in lone splendour hung aloft the night
And watching, with eternal lids apart,
Like nature's patient, sleepless Eremite,
The moving waters at their priestlike task
Of pure ablution round earth's human shores,
Or gazing on the new soft fallen mask
Of snow upon the mountains and the moors –
No – yet still steadfast, still unchangeable,
Pillow'd upon my fair love's ripening breast,
To feel for ever its soft fall and swell,
Awake for ever in a sweet unrest,
Still, still to hear her tender-taken breath,
And so live ever – or else swoon to death.

(*Sonnets* XX)

1 **steadfast:** standhaft, fest. – **art:** *are.* – 2 **lone** (poet.): *lonely.* – **aloft:** hoch oben auf, über. – 4 **eremite** (poet.): *hermit:* Eremit, Einsiedler. – 6 **ablution:** (rituelle) Waschung, Reinigung. – 10 **pillow'd:** gebettet (*pillow*: [Kopf-]Kissen). – 14 **to swoon:** ohnmächtig werden.

If thou must love me, let it be for nought
Except for love's sake only. Do not say
"I love her for her smile – her look – her way
Of speaking gently, – for a trick of thought
That falls in well with mine, and certes brought
A sense of pleasant ease on such a day" –
For these things in themselves, Beloved, may
Be changed, or change for thee, – and love, so wrought,
May be unwrought so. Neither love me for
Thine own dear pity's wiping my cheeks dry, –
A creature might forget to weep, who bore
Thy comfort long, and lose thy love thereby!
But love me for love's sake, that evermore
Thou mayst love on, through love's eternity.

(*Sonnets from the Portuguese* XIV)

1 **nought:** nichts. – 4 **trick:** Kunstgriff, Laune, Eigenart. – 5 **to fall in with s.th.:** zu etwas passen, mit etwas übereinstimmen. – **certes:** sicherlich, fürwahr. – 8 **wrought:** gemacht, gearbeitet, gewirkt. – 13 **evermore:** für immer, immerfort.

GEORGE MEREDITH

What are we first? First, animals; and next
Intelligences at a leap; on whom
Pale lies the distant shadow of the tomb,
And all that draweth on the tomb for text.
Into which state comes Love, the crowning sun:
Beneath whose light the shadow loses form.
We are the lords of life, and life is warm.
Intelligence and instinct now are one.
But nature says: "My children most they seem
When they least know me: therefore I decree
That they shall suffer." Swift doth young Love flee,
And we stand wakened, shivering from our dream.
Then if we study Nature we are wise.
Thus do the few who live but with the day:
The scientific animals are they. –
Lady, this is my sonnet to your eyes.

(*Modern Love* XXX)

4 **to draw on s.th.:** auf etwas Bezug nehmen. – **text:** Text, Motto, Thema. – 10 **to decree:** verfügen, anordnen. – 16 **sonnet:** Abweichend von der Konvention haben Merediths Sonette sechzehn Zeilen.

Lovesight

When do I see thee most, beloved one?
  When in the light the spirits of mine eyes
  Before thy face, their altar, solemnize
The worship of that Love through thee made known?
Or when in the dusk hours, (we two alone,)
  Close-kissed and eloquent of still replies
  Thy twilight-hidden glimmering visage lies,
And my soul only sees thy soul its own?

O love, my love! if I no more should see
Thyself, nor on the earth the shadow of thee,
  Nor image of thine eyes in any spring, –
How then should sound upon Life's darkening slope
The ground-whirl of the perished leaves of Hope,
  The wind of Death's imperishable wing?

(*The House of Life* IV)

3 **to solemnize** feiern, festlich begehen. – 7 **to glimmer:** schimmern. – **visage:** Angesicht, Antlitz. – 11 **spring:** Quelle, Brunnen.

CHRISTINA ROSSETTI

I wish I could remember that first day,
   First hour first moment of your meeting me,
   If bright or dim the season, it might be
Summer or Winter for aught I can say;
So unrecorded did it slip away,
   So blind was I to see and to foresee,
   So dull to mark the budding of my tree
That would not blossom yet for many a May.
If only I could recollect it, such
   A day of days! I let it come and go
   As traceless as a thaw of bygone snow;
It seemed to mean so little, meant so much;
If only now I could recall that touch,
   First touch of hand in hand – Did one but know!

(*Monna Innominata* II)

4 **for aught I can say:** soviel ich weiß; soviel ich zu sagen vermag. – 11 **thaw:** (Auf-)Tauen. – **bygone:** vergangen. – 13 **to recall s.th.:** sich an etwas erinnern.

A Church Romance

(Mellstock: circa 1835)

She turned in the high pew, until her sight
Swept the west gallery, and caught its row
Of music-men with viol, book, and bow
Against the sinking sad tower-window light.

She turned again; and in her pride's despite
One strenuous viol's inspirer seemed to throw
A message from his string to her below,
Which said: "I claim thee as my own forthright!"

Thus their hearts' bond began, in due time signed.
And long years thence, when Age had scared Romance,
At some old attitude of his or glance
That gallery-scene would break upon her mind,
With him as minstrel, ardent, young, and trim,
Bowing "New Sabbath" or "Mount Ephraim".

[Untertitel] **Mellstock:** Ort der ersten Begegnung zwischen Hardys Eltern, die 1839 geheiratet haben. – 1 **pew:** Kirchenstuhl, -bank. – 3 **viol:** Viola, Gambe. – 5 **in despite:** zum Trotz. – 6 **strenuous:** emsig, eifrig. – 8 **forthright:** aufrichtig, freimütig, geradewegs. – 12 **to break upon s.th.:** plötzlich über etwas hereinbrechen. – 13 **minstrel:** Spielmann, Musikant. – 14 **"New Sabbath" / "Mount Ephraim":** Titel von Kirchenliedern (*Ephraim*: Gebirge in Israel; Siedlungsgebiet des gleichnamigen israelitischen Stammes).

ALFRED EDWARD HOUSMAN

When I was one-and-twenty
  I heard a wise man say,
"Give crowns and pounds and guineas
  But not your heart away;
Give pearls away and rubies
  But keep your fancy free."
But I was one-and-twenty,
  No use to talk to me.

When I was one-and-twenty
  I heard him say again,
"The heart out of the bosom
  Was never given in vain;
'Tis paid with sighs a plenty
  And sold for endless rue."
And I am two-and-twenty,
  And oh, 'tis true, 'tis true.

(*A Shropshire Lad* XIII)

3 **guinea:** Guinee (Münze im Wert von 21 Schilling). – 5 **ruby:** Rubin. – 13 **a plenty:** in Fülle, im Überfluß. – 14 **rue** (obs.): Reue, Kummer.

The Rose of the World

Who dreamed that beauty passes like a dream?
For these red lips, with all their mournful pride,
Mournful that no new wonder may betide,
Troy passed away in one high funeral gleam,
And Usna's children died.

We and the labouring world are passing by:
Amid men's souls, that waver and give place
Like the pale waters in their wintry race,
Under the passing stars, foam of the sky,
Lives on this lonely face.

Bow down, archangels, in your dim abode:
Before you were, or any hearts to beat,
Weary and kind one lingered by His seat;
He made the world to be a grassy road
Before her wandering feet.

3 **to betide:** geschehen, widerfahren. – 4 **Troy:** Troja. – **gleam:** Schein, Licht-, Feuerstrahl. – 5 **Usna:** Gestalt der irischen Sage; Vater des Geliebten der Deirdre und seiner Brüder. Durch die Anspielung auf die Zerstörung Trojas und die Ermordung der Söhne Usnas identifiziert der Sprecher die Geliebte des Gedichtes mit Helena und Deirdre. – 11 **archangel:** Erzengel. – **abode:** Wohnung, Wohnsitz.

I so Liked Spring

I so liked Spring last year
    Because you were here; –
        The thrushes too –
Because it was these you so liked to hear –
        I so liked you.

    This year's a different thing, –
        I'll not think of you.
But I'll like Spring because it is simply Spring
        As the thrushes do.

3 **thrush:** Drossel.

Andraitx – Pomegranate Flowers

It is June, it is June
the pomegranates are in flower,
the peasants are bending cutting the bearded wheat.

The pomegranates are in flower
beside the high-road, past the deathly dust,
and even the sea is silent in the sun.

Short gasps of flame in the green of night, way off
the pomegranates are in flower,
small sharp red fires in the night of leaves.

And noon is suddenly dark, is lustrous, is silent and dark
men are unseen, beneath the shading hats;
only, from out the foliage of the secret loins
red flamelets here and there reveal
a man, a woman there.

[Titel] **Andraitx:** Ort auf Mallorca. – **pomegranate:** Granatapfel. – 10 **lustrous:** glänzend. – 12 **foliage:** Laubwerk. – **loin:** Lende. – 13 **flamelet:** Flämmchen.

A Channel Passage

The damned ship lurched and slithered. Quiet and quick
   My cold gorge rose; the long sea rolled; I knew
I must think hard of something, or be sick;
   And could think hard of only one thing – *you*!
You, you alone could hold my fancy ever!
   And with you memories come, sharp pain, and dole.
Now there's a choice – heartache or tortured liver!
   A sea-sick body, or a you-sick soul!

Do I forget you? Retchings twist and tie me,
   Old meat, good meals, brown gobbets, up I throw.
Do I remember? Acrid return and slimy,
   The sobs and slobber of a last year's woe.
And still the sick ship rolls. 'Tis hard, I tell ye,
To choose 'twixt love and nausea, heart and belly.

1 **to lurch:** schlingern. – **to slither:** gleiten, schlittern. – 2 **my gorge rose:** mir wurde übel (*gorge:* Kehle). – 3 **to be sick:** sich übergeben. – 6 **dole:** Kummer. – 7 **liver:** Leber. – 9 **retching:** Würgen, Erbrechen. – 10 **gobbet:** Brocken, Stück. – **to throw up:** erbrechen. – 11 **acrid:** scharf, beißend. – **slimy:** schleimig. – 12 **slobber:** Geifer. – 14 **nausea:** Übelkeit, Brechreiz; Seekrankheit.

Never Such Love

Twined together and, as is customary,
For words of rapture groping, they
“Never such love,” swore, “ever before was!”
Contrast with all loves that had failed or staled
Registered their own as love indeed.

And was this not to blab idly
The heart’s fated inconstancy?
Better in love to seal the love-sure lips,
For truly love was before words were,
And no word given, no word broken.

When the name “love” is uttered
(Love, the near-honourable malady
With which in greed and haste they
Each other do infect and curse)
Or, worse, is written down. . . .

Wise after the event, by love withered,
A “never more!” most frantically
Sorrow and shame would proclaim
Such as, they’d swear, never before were:
True lovers even in this.

1 **to twine:** (ineinander) verschlingen, zusammendrehen, winden. – 2 **rapture:** Entzücken. – **to grope:** tasten, tastend suchen. – 4 **to stale:** schal werden. – 6 **to blab:** plappern, schwätzen. – 7 **fated:** (vom Schicksal) bestimmt. – 12 **malady:** Krankheit.

EDMUND BLUNDEN

Lonely Love

I love to see those loving and beloved
Whom Nature seems to have spited; unattractive,
Unnoticeable people, whose dry track
No honey-drop of praise, or understanding,
Or bare acknowledgment that they existed,
Perhaps yet moistened. Still, they make their world.

She with her arm in his – O Fate, be kind,
Though late, be kind; let her have never cause
To live outside her dream, nor unadore
This underling in body, mind and type,
Nor part from him what makes her dwarfish form
Take grace and fortune, envy's antitone.

I saw where through the plain a river and road
Ran quietly, and asked no more event
Than sun and rain and wind, and night and day,
Two walking – from what cruel show escaped?
Deformity, defect of mind their portion.
But I forget the rest of that free day of mine,
And in what flowerful coils, what airy music
It led me there and on; those two I see
Who, loving, walking slowly, saw not me,
But shared with me the strangest happiness.

2 **to spite s.o.:** jdn. kränken, jdm. eins auswischen. – 10 **underling:** Untergebene(r), Untergeordnete(r). – 11 **dwarfish:** zwergenhaft. – 12 **antitone:** Gegenton, -stimmung, -kraft. – 17 **deformity:** Mißgestalt. – 19 **coil:** Windung.

A Subaltern's Love-song

Miss J. Hunter Dunn, Miss J. Hunter Dunn,
Furnish'd and burnish'd by Aldershot sun,
What strenuous singles we played after tea,
We in the tournament – you against me!

Love-thirty, love-forty, oh! weakness of joy,
The speed of a swallow, the grace of a boy,
With carefullest carelessness, gaily you won,
I am weak from your loveliness, Joan Hunter Dunn.

Miss Joan Hunter Dunn, Miss Joan Hunter Dunn,
How mad I am, sad I am, glad that you won.
The warm-handled racket is back in its press,
But my shock-headed victor, she loves me no less.

Her father's euonymus shines as we walk,
And swing past the summer-house, buried in talk,
And cool the verandah that welcomes us in
To the six-o'clock news and a lime-juice and gin.

The scent of the conifers, sound of the bath,
The view from my bedroom of moss-dappled path,

[Titel] **subaltern:** Subalterner; (Ober-)Leutnant. – 2 **furnish'd:** 1. ausgestattet; 2. (obs.) verschönert. – **burnish'd:** glänzend gemacht, brüniert gebräunt. – **Aldershot:** Garnisonsstadt südwestlich von London. – 3 **strenuous:** eifrig, anstrengend. – 4 **tournament:** Turnier. – 5 **love-thirty:** null dreißig (Tennis). – 11 **racket:** (Tennis-)Schläger. – **press:** (Schläger-)Spanner. – 12 **shock-headed:** strubblig. – 13 **euonymus:** Spindelbaum, Obstbaum mit kurzen Seitenästen. – 16 **lime-juice:** Limonensaft. – 17 **conifer:** Konifere, Nadelbaum. – 18 **moss-dappled:** moosgesprenkelt, mit Moosflecken.

As I struggle with double-end evening tie,
For we dance at the Golf Club, my victor and I.

On the floor of her bedroom lie blazer and shorts
And the cream-coloured walls are be-trophied with sports,
And westering, questioning settles the sun
On your low-leaded window, Miss Joan Hunter Dunn.

The Hillman is waiting, the light's in the hall,
The pictures of Egypt are bright on the wall,
My sweet, I am standing beside the oak stair
And there on the landing's the light on your hair.

By roads "not adopted", by woodlanded ways,
She drove to the club in the late summer haze,
Into nine-o'clock Camberley, heavy with bells
And mushroomy, pine-woody, evergreen smells.

Miss Joan Hunter Dunn, Miss Joan Hunter Dunn,
I can hear from the car-park the dance has begun.
Oh! full Surrey twilight! importunate band!
Oh! strongly adorable tennis-girl's hand!

Around us are Rovers and Austins afar,
Above us, the intimate roof of the car,
And here on my right is the girl of my choice,
With the tilt of her nose and the chime of her voice,

23 **westering:** nach Westen wandernd. – 24 **low-leaded:** niedrig und bleiverglast. – 25 **Hillman:** Automarke. – 28 **landing:** Treppenabsatz. – 29 **adopted:** hier: gepflegt, instand gehalten. – 30 **haze:** Dunst, leichter Nebel. – 31 **Camberley:** südenglische Stadt in der Grafschaft Surrey, in der Nähe von Aldershot gelegen. – 32 **pine-woody:** von Nadelholz. – **evergreen:** immergrüne Pflanze. – 35 **importunate:** lästig, aufdringlich. – 40 **tilt:** Neigung, Aufwärtsbiegung. – **chime:** Glockenklang.

And the scent of her wrap, and the words never said,
And the ominous, ominous dancing ahead.
We sat in the car park till twenty to one
And now I'm engaged to Miss Joan Hunter Dunn.

41 **wrap:** Umschlagtuch, Schal. – 42 **ominous:** ominös, verhängnisvoll.

W. H. AUDEN

My second thoughts condemn
And wonder how I dare
To look you in the eye.
What right have I to swear
Even at one a.m.
To love you till I die?

Earth meets too many crimes
For fibs to interest her;
If I can give my word,
Forgiveness can recur
Any number of times
In Time. Which is absurd.

Tempus fugit. Quite.
So finish up your drink.
All flesh is grass. It is.
But who on earth can think
With heavy heart or light
Of what will come of this?

(*Twelve Songs* IX)

8 **fib:** Flunkerei, Schwindelei. – 10 **to recur:** zurückkommen, wiederkehren. – 13 **tempus fugit** (Lat.): die Zeit flieht (Vergil, *Georgica* 3,284). – 15 **all flesh is grass:** Jesaja 40,6.

An Arundel Tomb

Side by side, their faces blurred,
The earl and countess lie in stone,
Their proper habits vaguely shown
As jointed armour, stiffened pleat,
And that faint hint of the absurd –
The little dogs under their feet.

Such plainness of the pre-baroque
Hardly involves the eye, until
It meets his left-hand gauntlet, still
Clasped empty in the other; and
One sees, with a sharp tender shock,
His hand withdrawn, holding her hand.

They would not think to lie so long.
Such faithfulness in effigy
Was just a detail friends would see:
A sculptor's sweet commissioned grace
Thrown off in helping to prolong
The Latin names around the base.

They would not guess how early in
Their supine stationary voyage
The air would change to soundless damage,

[Titel] **Arundel:** Grafengeschlecht mit Sitz in der gleichnamigen Normannenburg in Sussex. – 1 **blurred:** verwischt, verschwommen, entstellt. – 4 **jointed:** mit Gelenken. – **pleat:** (Stoff-)Falte. – 9 **gauntlet:** (Panzer-, Stulpen-)Handschuh. – 14 **effigy:** Abbild, figürliche Nachbildung. – 16 **commissioned:** in Auftrag gegeben. – 18 **base:** Sockel. – 20 **supine:** hingestreckt, auf dem Rücken liegend.

Turn the old tenantry away;
How soon succeeding eyes begin
To look, not read. Rigidly they

Persisted, linked, through lengths and breadths
Of time. Snow fell, undated. Light
Each summer thronged the glass. A bright
Litter of birdcalls strewed the same
Bone-riddled ground. And up the paths
The endless altered people came,

Washing at their identity.
Now, helpless in the hollow of
An unarmorial age, a trough
Of smoke in slow suspended skeins
Above their scrap of history,
Only an attitude remains:

Time has transfigured them into
Untruth. The stone fidelity
They hardly meant has come to be
Their final blazon, and to prove
Our almost-instinct almost true:
What will survive of us is love.

22 **tenantry:** Pächter(schaft). – 27 **to throng:** füllen, überfluten. – 28 **to strew:** bestreuen, bedecken. – 29 **bone-riddled:** von Knochen durchsetzt. – 33 **unarmorial:** unheraldisch, wappenlos. – **trough:** Trog, Rinne, Mulde. – 34 **skein:** Strähne, Strang, Fadengewirr. – 37 **to transfigure:** umgestalten, verwandeln. – 40 **blazon:** Wappenschild, heraldische Erklärung.

Winter Love

Let us have winter loving that the heart
May be in peace and ready to partake
Of the slow pleasure spring would wish to hurry
Or that in summer harshly would awake,
And let us fall apart, O gladly weary,
The white skin shaken like a white snowflake.

2f. **to partake of s.th.:** an etwas teilhaben.

THOM GUNN

During an Absence

I used to think that obstacles to love
  Were out of date, the darkened stairs
Leading deprived ones to the mossy tomb
Where she lay carpeted with golden hairs:
  We had no place in such a room,
Belonging to the common ground above.

In sunlight we are free to move, and hold
  Our open assignations, yet
Each love defines its proper obstacles:
Our frowning Montague and Capulet
  Are air, not individuals
And have no faces for their frowns to fold.

Even in sunlight what does freedom mean?
  Romeo's passion rose to fire
From one thin spark within a brace of days.
We for whom time draws out, visas expire,
  Smoulder without a chance to blaze
Upon the unities of a paper scene.

The violence of a picturesque account
  Gives way to details none the less
Reaching, each one more narrow than the last,
Down to a separate hygienic place

8 **assignation:** Treffen (bes. eines Liebespaares). – 10 **Montague and Capulet:** Namen der verfeindeten Familien in Shakespeares *Romeo and Juliet*. – 15 **a brace of:** ein Paar, zwei. – 16 **to draw out:** länger werden, sich in die Länge ziehen. – **to expire:** ablaufen, auslaufen. – 17 **to smoulder:** glimmen, schwelen.

Where acting love is in the past,
No golden hairs are there, no bleeding count.

No, if there were bright things to fasten on
There'd be no likeness to the play.
But under a self-generated glare
Any bad end has possibility,
The means endurance. I declare
I know how hard upon the ground it shone.

27 **self-generated:** selbst erzeugt, selbst verursacht. – 29 **endurance:** Ausdauer, Dauer.

September

We sit late, watching the dark slowly unfold:
No clock counts this.
When kisses are repeated and the arms hold
There is no telling where time is.

It is midsummer: the leaves hang big and still:
Behind the eye a star,
Under the silk of the wrist a sea, tell
Time is nowhere.

We stand; leaves have not timed the summer.
No clock now needs
Tell we have only what we remember:
Minutes uproaring with our heads

Like an unfortunate King's and his Queen's
When the senseless mob rules;
And quietly the trees casting their crowns
Into the pools.

12 **to uproar:** Aufruhr verursachen, Tumult veranstalten. – 14 **senseless:** gefühllos, unvernünftig. – **mob:** Pöbel.

Love Letter

Not easy to state the change you made.
If I'm alive now, then I was dead,
Though, like a stone, unbothered by it,
Staying put according to habit.
You didn't just toe me an inch, no –
Nor leave me to set my small bald eye
Skyward again, without hope, of course,
Of apprehending blueness, or stars.

That wasn't it. I slept, say: a snake
Masked among black rocks as a black rock
In the white hiatus of winter –
Like my neighbors, taking no pleasure
In the million perfectly-chiseled
Cheeks alighting each moment to melt
My cheek of basalt. They turned to tears,
Angels weeping over dull natures,
But didn't convince me. Those tears froze.
Each dead head had a visor of ice.

And I slept on like a bent finger.
The first thing I saw was sheer air
And the locked drops rising in a dew
Limpid as spirits. Many stones lay
Dense and expressionless round about.
I didn't know what to make of it.

5 **to toe:** mit den Fußspitzen anstoßen. – 6 **bald:** kahl. – 11 **hiatus:** Spalt, Lücke, Zwischenraum. – 13 **perfectly-chiseled:** perfekt gemeißelt, geformt. – 14 **to alight:** sich niederlassen, niedergehen. – 18 **visor:** Visier. – 22 **limpid:** klar, durchsichtig.

I shone, mica-scaled and unfolded
To pour myself out like a fluid
Among bird feet and the stems of plants.
I wasn't fooled. I knew you at once.

Tree and stone glittered, without shadows.
My finger-length grew lucent as glass.
I started to bud like a March twig:
An arm and a leg, an arm, a leg.
From stone to cloud, so I ascended.
Now I resemble a sort of god
Floating through the air in my soul-shift
Pure as a pane of ice. It's a gift.

25 **mica-scaled:** glimmergeschuppt, mit einer Schale, mit Schuppen aus Glimmer. – 28 **fooled:** getäuscht, betrogen, zum Narren gehalten. – 30 **lucent:** glänzend, klar, durchsichtig. – 35 **soul-shift:** Veränderung, Wechsel der Seele.

Comeclose and Sleepnow

it is afterwards
and you talk on tiptoe
happy to be part
of the darkness
lips becoming limp
a prelude to tiredness.
Comeclose and Sleepnow
for in the morning
when a policeman
disguised as the sun
creeps into the room
and your mother
disguised as birds
calls from the trees
you will put on a dress of guilt
and shoes with broken high ideals
and refusing coffee
run
alltheway
home.

2 **on tiptoe:** auf Zehenspitzen. – 5 **limp:** schlaff, weich. – 6 **prelude** Vorspiel.

Poem

For Marie

Love, I shall perfect for you the child
Who diligently potters in my brain
Digging with heavy spade till sods were piled
Or puddling through muck in a deep drain.

Yearly I would sow my yard-long garden.
I'd strip a layer of sods to build the wall
That was to exclude sow and pecking hen.
Yearly, admitting these, the sods would fall.

Or in the sucking clabber I would splash
Delightedly and dam the flowing drain
But always my bastions of clay and mush
Would burst before the rising autumn rain.

Love, you shall perfect for me this child
Whose small imperfect limits would keep breaking:
Within new limits now, arrange the world
Within our walls, within our golden ring.

diligently (adv.): emsig, eifrig. – **to potter:** herumwerkeln, -hantieren. – 3 **sod:** Rasenstück. – 4 **to puddle:** herumplantschen, -waten. – **muck:** Dreck. – **drain:** Rinne, Gosse, Graben. – 6 **layer:** Lage, Schicht. – 7 **sow:** Sau. – **to peck:** hacken, picken. – 9 **clabber:** Schlamm, Matsch. – 11 **mush:** Brei.

DOUGLAS DUNN

Modern Love

It is summer, and we are in a house
That is not ours, sitting at a table
Enjoying minutes of a rented silence,
The upstairs people gone. The pigeons lull
To sleep the under-tens and invalids,
The tree shakes out its shadows to the grass,
The roses rove through the wilds of my neglect.
Our lives flap, and we have no hope of better
happiness than this, not much to show for love
But how we are, or how this evening is,
Unpeopled, silent, and where we are alive
In a domestic love, seemingly alone,
All other lives worn down to trees and sunlight,
Looking forward to a visit from the cat.

4 **to lull:** einlullen. – 7 **to rove:** (umher)streifen. – **wilds** (pl.): Wildnis. – 8 **to flap:** flattern, baumeln. – 13 **to wear down:** abnutzen, verkleinern, reduzieren.

CAROL ANN DUFFY

Hard to Say

I asked him to give me an image for Love, something I could see,
or imagine seeing, or something that, because of the word
for its smell, would make me remember, something possible
to hear. *Don't just say love*, I said, *love, love, I love you.*

On the way home, I thought of our love and how, lately,
I too have grown lazy in expressing it, snuggling up to you
in bed, idly murmuring those tired clichés without even thinking.
My words have been grubby confetti, faded, tacky, blown far

from the wedding feast. And so it was, with a sudden shock of love,
like a peacock flashing wide its hundred eyes, or a boy's voice
flinging top G to the roof of an empty church, or a bottle
of French perfume knocked off the shelf, spilling into the steamy bath,

I wanted you. After the wine, the flowers I brought you drowned
in the darkening light. As we slept, we breathed their scent all night.

6 **to snuggle up to s.o.:** sich an jdn. anschmiegen, kuscheln. – 8 **grubby:** schmuddelig, schmutzig. – **tacky:** klebrig, schäbig, verkommen. – 10 **peacock:** Pfau. – 12 **to spill:** auslaufen, sich ergießen.

Editorische Notiz

Das Glossar erklärt in der Regel alle Wörter, die über die Wertigkeitsstufe 4 des *Englischen Arbeitswörterbuches* von Alfred Haase (Frankfurt a. M.: Moritz Diesterweg, [7]1979) hinausgehen. Im Zweifelsfall wurde großzügig verfahren, d. h. eher eine Vokabel mehr aufgenommen als dort vorgesehen. Die Gedichte sind unabhängig voneinander glossiert.
Bei den älteren Gedichten ist die Orthographie der jeweiligen Quellen-Edition beibehalten.

Im Glossar verwendete Abkürzungen

adv.	adverb
Lat.	Latin
obs.	obsolete (nicht mehr gebräuchlich)
o.s.	oneself
pl.	plural
poet.	poetical (dichterisch, gehoben)
s.o.	someone
s.th.	something

Zu den Autoren und Gedichten

Die Literaturhinweise geben – sofern vorhanden – Einzelinterpretationen zu den vorliegenden Gedichten an. Bei häufig interpretierten Gedichten wurde eine Auswahl getroffen. Wo keine Interpretation vorliegt, werden Titel genannt, die sich mit der Gedichtsequenz, der das hier abgedruckte Gedicht angehört, befassen oder es im Zusammenhang mit anderen Gedichten erwähnen. Bei Sekundärliteratur, die sich allgemein mit dem Werk des Autors befaßt, ohne auf das vorliegende Gedicht einzugehen, wurde dies vermerkt.

WYSTAN HUGH AUDEN

21. 2. 1907 York – 29. 9. 1973 Wien

W. H. Auden ist einer der bedeutendsten englischsprachigen Dichter dieses Jahrhunderts. Als Sohn einer Krankenschwester und eines Arztes entwickelte er zunächst Interesse für Naturwissenschaften, studierte dann aber in Oxford Politik, Philosophie und englische Literatur. Nach längerem Aufenthalt in Berlin arbeitete er zunächst als Lehrer, dann als freier Schriftsteller. In den dreißiger Jahren war er die profilierteste Gestalt einer Gruppe literarisch bedeutender, linksorientierter junger Dichter in Oxford. Kurzzeitig war er mit Erika Mann verheiratet. Längere Reisen führten ihn quer durch Europa, auch nach Island und China; während des Bürgerkrieges in Spanien war er dort als Krankenwagenfahrer beschäftigt. Seine frühen Gedichte waren technisch brillant und innovatorisch sowie politisch engagiert, zunehmend auch von psychologischem Interesse gekennzeichnet. Immer wieder wird die Neigung zur Bearbeitung abstrakter Probleme deutlich, die in bildhaft-sinnliche Darstellungen eingebunden werden, so auch in »My second thoughts condemn« oder in dem berühmten, fünf Jahre früher geschriebenen Liebesgedicht »Lullaby«. 1939 wanderte Auden in die USA aus; eines seiner zentralen Bilder, das des Wanderers, der auf der Suche ist nach Ordnung, Sinn und Ziel, scheint hier im selbstgewählten Exil eine biographische Entsprechung zu finden. Seine innere Entwicklung richtete sich nach der Abkehr vom Sozialismus auf die christliche Religion. Zu den Höhepunkten seines Werkes zählt das lange Gedicht *The Age of*

Anxiety (1948), das von der Heillosigkeit der Welt aufgrund von Schuld und daraus resultierender Angst handelt. Die Vielfalt der Themen und Formen, die Auden erfolgreich handhabte, veranlaßte den Kritiker Kenneth Allott zu der Feststellung, seinesgleichen sei in der Literatur nicht zu finden, wohl aber in der bildenden Kunst, in der Vielfalt Picassos.

Text: *Collected Shorter Poems 1927–1957*, London: Faber and Faber, 1966. Reprinted by permission of Faber and Faber Ltd, London.

Sekundärliteratur: John Fuller, *A Reader's Guide to W. H. Auden*, New York 1970, S. 175; George Sutherland Fraser, *Essays on Twentieth Century Poets*, Leicester: Leicester University Press, 1977. (Nicht zu »My second thoughts condemn«.)

BARRETT BROWNING → BROWNING

(SIR) JOHN BETJEMAN

28. 8. 1906 Highgate (London) – 19. 5. 1984 Trebetherick (Cornwall)

John Betjeman entstammte einer wohlhabenden Kaufmannsfamilie. Er verbrachte seine Kindheit in einem eleganten Londoner Vorort, besuchte eine Public School und studierte in Oxford, wo er sich der tonangebenden Gruppe der Studenten aus besseren Kreisen anschloß, die sein Freund Evelyn Waugh später in seinen Romanen charakterisierte. Während des Krieges arbeitete er im Informationsministerium und lernte dort das Mädchen kennen, das zum Vorbild für »Miss Joan Hunter Dunn« wurde. Das Bewußtsein der Klassenzugehörigkeit begleitete ihn sein Leben lang und festigte seine Stellung in der englischen Gesellschaft, die ihm reichlich Anerkennung zollte bis hin zu seiner Erhebung in den Ritterstand (1969) und seiner Ernennung zum »poet laureate« (1972). Dennoch wäre es verfehlt, Betjeman als einen Modedichter zu bezeichnen. In der Literaturkritik ist sein Ansehen geteilt; während er bei einigen gerade wegen seiner Popularität als mittelmäßig gilt, wird er von anderen, unter ihnen Philip Larkin, hoch geschätzt. Ein wesentliches Merkmal seiner Dichtung ist die Verwurzelung im Traditionellen, die Liebe zum Viktorianischen, die sanfte Satire auf das moderne England. In ihrer Schlichtheit und Leichtigkeit verweist sie vielfach auf existentielle Nöte, die sich hinter Alltagserfahrungen verbergen. Betjemans zweite große Neigung galt der Architektur. Auch hier gehörte sein Interesse dem 19. Jahrhundert, auch hier kritisierte er die Geistlosigkeit und Häßlichkeit seiner eigenen Epoche.

Text: *John Betjeman's Collected Poems*, London: John Murray, 1970. Reprinted by permission of John Murray (Publishers) Ltd, London.

Sekundärliteratur: Patrick Taylor-Martin, *John Betjeman. His Life and Work*, London 1983. S. 97 f.

WILLIAM BLAKE

28. 11. 1757 London – 12. 8. 1827 London

Blakes Vater erkannte früh die künstlerische Neigung seines Sohnes und schickte ihn schon als Zehnjährigen auf eine Zeichenschule und einige Jahre später in die Lehre zu dem Kupferstecher James Basire. Anschließend besuchte William die Londoner Royal Academy. Ebenfalls noch im Kindesalter begann er Verse zu schreiben. Er verdiente sein Geld mit Buchillustrationen. Als er für seine eigenen *Songs of Innocence* keinen Verleger fand, brachte er sie in einer handgefertigten Ausgabe heraus. Zusammen mit den *Songs of Experience* gehören sie dichterisch wie künstlerisch zu seinen besten Werken. Blakes visionäre Kraft führte ihn mehr und mehr zu prophetischer Dichtung, einer selbstgeschaffenen Mythologie voll rätselhafter Symbolik, während er sich in der bildenden Kunst, als Kupferstecher wie auch als Maler, vielfach Motiven aus der Bibel, aus der *Göttlichen Komödie* und der englischen Literatur zuwandte.

Text: *The Complete Writings of William Blake*, edited by Geoffrey Keynes, London: Oxford University Press, 1966.

Sekundärliteratur: Jean H. Hagstrum, »William Blake's ›The Clod & the Pebble‹«, in: Carroll Camden (Hrsg.), *Restoration and Eighteenth-Century Literature*, Chicago 1963, S. 381–388; Max F. Schulz, »Point of View in Blake's ›The Clod and the Pebble‹«, in: *Papers on Language and Literature* 2 (Sommer 1966) S. 217–224; Wolf Mankowitz, »The ›Songs of Experience‹«, in: Margaret Bottrall (Hrsg.), *William Blake. Songs of Innocence and Experience. A Casebook*, London 1970, S. 123–135; Northrop Frye, »Blake's Introduction to Experience«, in: N. F. (Hrsg.), *Blake. A Collection of Critical Essays*, Englewood Cliffs (N. J.) 1966, S. 23–31.

EDMUND BLUNDEN

1.11.1896 London – 20.1.1974 Long Melford (Suffolk)

Edmund Blunden war das erste von neun Kindern einer Lehrerfamilie. Er wuchs in dem Dorf Yalding in Kent auf und besuchte eine Grammar School. 1914 wurden erstmals Gedichte von ihm veröffentlicht, deren vorherrschendes Thema die Natur und das Leben des Menschen in der Natur war. Unter dem Einfluß seines Wehrdienstes in Frankreich und Belgien thematisierte er Kriegsereignisse. Nach einem kurzen Aufenthalt am Queen's College, Oxford, widmete Blunden sich überwiegend der Dichtung sowie dem literarischen Journalismus und schrieb mehrere Biographien. Private Reisen und Lehraufträge führten ihn nach Südamerika, Hong Kong und Tokio, wo er auch für einige Zeit als Diplomat arbeitete. 1964 kehrte er nach England zurück. Blundens Dichtung, die sich neben der Natur zunehmend auch philosophischen Fragestellungen zuwandte, ist in der Form traditionell und läßt Einflüsse des 18. Jahrhunderts und der Romantik erkennen.

Text: *Poems of Many Years*, London: Collins, 1957. Reprinted by permission of International Literary Agency, London.

Sekundärliteratur: Thomas Mallon, *Edmund Blunden*, Boston 1983, S. 83.

RUPERT BROOKE

3.8.1887 Rugby – 23.4.1915 vor Skiros (Griechenland)

Rupert Brooke galt zum Zeitpunkt seines Todes als eines der bedeutendsten lyrischen Talente, er wurde zur Symbolfigur der durch den Krieg zerstörten jungen Generation. Er war der Sohn eines Schuldirektors und kam früh mit Literatur in Berührung, bereits mit neun Jahren schrieb er erste eigene Gedichte. Gleichzeitig war er voller Vitalität und Energie, ein guter Schüler und hervorragender Sportler, ein strahlender junger Mann, den Yeats als den schönsten Jüngling Englands pries. Brooke studierte in Cambridge und stand zeitweise in Beziehung zur Bloomsbury Group. Seine literarischen Vorbilder waren neben den Dichtern der Jahrhundertwende die Romantiker Shelley und Keats. Sein erster und einziger zu Lebzeiten veröffentlichter Lyrikband erschien 1911, darin auch »A Channel Passage«, das ursprünglich »Shakespearean Love Sonnet« heißen sollte. Viele seiner frühen Gedichte tragen noch den Charakter literarischer Übungen, in denen abstraktes Gedankengut und konkrete Bildlichkeit keine hinreichende Verbindung eingehen. Brooke unternahm mehrere Reisen durch Europa, nach Nordamerika und in die Südsee. 1914 trat er in die Marine ein und tat zunächst Kriegsdienst in Belgien. In dieser Zeit entstanden einige seiner bekanntesten Sonette, in denen der Krieg noch in patriotischem Licht gesehen wird, anders als bei den »war poets« der letzten Kriegsjahre, die von der Grausamkeit und dem Leid ihrer Erfahrungen geprägt sind. Auf dem Gallipoli-Feldzug starb Brooke an den Folgen einer Blutvergiftung.

Text: *The Complete Poems*, New York: AMS Press, 1977.

Sekundärliteratur: Armin Geraths, »Rupert Brooke. ›A Channel Passage‹«, in: Karl Heinz Göller (Hrsg.), *Die englische Lyrik II. Von der Renaissance zur Gegenwart,* Düsseldorf 1968, S. 288–298.

ELIZABETH BARRETT BROWNING

6.3.1806 Coxhoe Hall (Durham) – 29.6.1861 Florenz

Elizabeth Barrett verbrachte eine glückliche Kindheit auf dem Anwesen ihres Vaters in Hertfordshire. Sie war ein frühreifes Kind, das Privatunterricht bekam und schon mit acht Jahren Homer auf griechisch las, gleichzeitig aber liebte sie die Natur und ritt leidenschaftlich gern. Fünfzehnjährig hatte sie dabei einen Unfall und verletzte sich die Wirbelsäule, so daß sie jahrelang liegen mußte. Durch den Tod ihres Bruders wurde ihre schwache Konstitution weiter erschüttert. Sie blieb kränklich und konnte das Haus kaum verlassen. Während dieser Zeit schrieb sie Gedichte und Essays. Trotz ihrer Zurückgezogenheit fand sie große Beachtung in literarischen Kreisen. 1846 heiratete sie den Dichter Robert Browning. Ihm widmete sie die *Sonnets from the Portuguese*, ihre schönsten Gedichte. Ihrer Gesundheit wegen zog das Ehepaar nach Florenz. Elizabeth Barrett Browning interessierte sich zunehmend für die politischen Geschicke ihrer Wahlheimat Italien, die sie in ihren späteren Gedichten thematisierte.

Text: *The Complete Works of Elizabeth Barrett Browning*, Vol. 3, edited with introduction and notes by Charlotte Porter and Helen A. Clarke, New York: AMS Press, 1973.

Sekundärliteratur: Ruth Freifrau von Ledebur, »Elizabeth Barrett Browning. ›If thou must love me‹«, in: Reinhold Schiffer / Hermann J. Weiand (Hrsg.), *Insight III. Analyses of English and American Poetry*, Frankfurt 1972, S. 50–53; Angela Leighton, *Elizabeth Barrett Browning*, Brighton 1986, S. 75–113; Dorothy Mermin, »The Female Poet and the Embarrassed Reader: Elizabeth Barrett Browning's *Sonnets from the Portuguese*«, in: *Journal of English Literary History* 48 (1981) S. 351–367.

ROBERT BURNS

25.1.1759 Alloway (Ayrshire) – 21.7.1796 Dumfries

Robert Burns war das älteste von sieben Kindern einer wenig begüterten Bauernfamilie. Er konnte nur unregelmäßig die Schule besuchen, wurde teilweise von seinem Vater unterrichtet und erwarb sich den größten Teil seiner Bildung, einschließlich Kenntnissen der französischen und lateinischen Sprache, als Autodidakt. Aufgrund finanzieller Probleme und der in ihrer Gültigkeit umstrittenen Ehe mit Jean Armour wollte er nach Jamaika auswandern. Die Veröffentlichung seiner ersten Gedichte sollte ihm das notwendige Geld für die Schiffspassage einbringen. Nach dem Erfolg der Sammlung ließ er das Auswanderungsprojekt fallen. Sein weiteres Leben war gekennzeichnet durch wenig erfolgreiche Arbeit als Bauer, durch lebenslustige gesellschaftliche Aktivitäten bis hin zu alkoholischen Exzessen, durch freimaurerische Betätigung und heftige Satiren gegen die orthodoxe Theologie – wobei er aber den schlichten Glauben der bäuerlichen Bevölkerung immer respektierte –, durch vielfältige leidenschaftliche Beziehungen zu Frauen, trotz der erneuten und kirchlich bestätigten Eheschließung mit Jean Armour, und vor allem durch ein äußerst produktives dichterisches Schaffen, das auch das Sammeln und teilweise Umgestalten alter schottischer Volkslieder einschloß. Einige seiner Gedichte, wie »Auld lang syne«, sind selbst zu Volksliedern geworden.

Text: *The Poems and Songs of Robert Burns*, Vol. 2, edited by James Kinsley, Oxford: Clarendon Press, 1968.

Sekundärliteratur: M. E. B. Lewis, »What To Do with ›A Red, Red Rose‹. A New Category of Burns's Songs«, in: *Scottish Literary Journal* 3, Heft 2 (1976) S. 62–75.

GEORGE GORDON LORD BYRON

22.1.1788 London – 19.4.1824 Mesolongion (Griechenland)

George Gordon Byron, dessen Vater früh starb, verbrachte seine Kindheit mit seiner Mutter in Aberdeen. 1794 erbte er den Titel und das Vermögen seines Großonkels und konnte daraufhin die Public School in Harrow und die Universität Cambridge besuchen. Das Studium sagte ihm nicht sonderlich zu; trotz einer Behinderung am Fuß war er mehr dem Sport zugeneigt, jedoch las er unersättlich. 1806 erschien ein erster Band seiner Gedichte. Byron bezog unterdessen das ererbte, aber weitgehend verfallene Haus Newstead Abbey. 1809 brach er zu einer zweijährigen Reise durch Südeuropa auf. Nach England zurückgekehrt, brachte ihm die Veröffentlichung des epischen Gedichtes *Childe Harold's Pilgrimage* Anerkennung; die Gesellschaft bewunderte ihn als einen faszinierenden und exzentrischen jungen Helden. Verschiedene Skandale – Liebschaften und das Gerücht des Inzestes – und eine kurze, in Scheidung endende Ehe ließen ihn aber 1816 erneut und für immer zum Kontinent aufbrechen. »When we two parted«, 1815 geschrieben, wurde von ihm selbst um sieben Jahre vordatiert, vermutlich um die Identität der Adressatin, einer verheirateten Dame der Gesellschaft, zu verschleiern. In Italien entstand sein Hauptwerk, das satirische Versepos *Don Juan*, das unvollendet blieb. Auf der Suche nach einer neuen, außerhalb der Literatur liegenden Aufgabe engagierte er sich im Freiheitskampf der Griechen gegen die Türken.

Text: *The Complete Poetical Works*, Vol. 3, edited by Jerome J. McGann, Oxford: Clarendon Press, 1981.

Sekundärliteratur: Jerome J. McGann, »The Significance of Biographical Context«, in: Louis L. Martz / Aubrey Williams, *The Author in His Work*, New Haven / London 1978, S. 347–364; Hans Banek, »George Gordon Lord Byron, ›When we two parted‹«, in: Reinhold Schiffer / Hermann J. Weiand (Hrsg.), *Insight III. Analyses of English and American Poetry*, Frankfurt 1972, S. 60–65.

JOHN CLARE

13.7.1793 Helpston (Northampshire) – 20.5.1864 Northampton

John Clare war der Sohn einfacher Landarbeiter, die kaum lesen und nicht schreiben konnten. Seine eigene Schulbildung war fragmentarisch und wurde immer wieder von der Notwendigkeit unterbrochen, auf dem Feld zu helfen. Dennoch konnte er sich im Selbststudium erstaunliche Kenntnisse erwerben. Er war jedoch kein Bücherwurm, sondern sah in seiner Lebenserfahrung, die durch eine ausgeprägte Beobachtungsgabe gefördert wurde, einen wesentlichen Teil seiner Bildung. Noch während seiner Schulzeit verliebte er sich in eine Bauerntochter, die lebenslang als Idealbild der Frau in seiner Dichtung erscheint. Nach verschiedenen Beschäftigungen als Gärtner oder landwirtschaftlicher Gehilfe ging er aus finanziellen Gründen und ohne Liebe zur Sache zum Militär. Finanzielle Sorgen bestimmten auch sein weiteres Leben, insbesondere nach seiner Heirat und der Geburt von acht Kindern. Seine Gedichte, deren ersten Band er 1820 veröffentlichte, brachten ihm nur in geringem Maß Geld und Anerkennung. Der Titel der ersten Sammlung *Poems Descriptive of Rural Life and Scenery* verweist auf die vorherrschende Thematik seiner Dichtung, das ländliche England vor der industriellen Revolution. Psychische Belastungen und Krankheiten führten zu einem Zusammenbruch und zunehmender geistiger Verwirrung, so daß Clare das letzte Drittel seines Lebens in einer Anstalt verbringen mußte. Sein dichterisches Werk wurde erst im 20. Jahrhundert, insbesondere durch Edmund Blunden, wiederentdeckt und gewürdigt.

Text: *The Poems of John Clare*, Vol. 1, edited with an introduction by J. W. Tibble, London: Dent, 1935.

Sekundärliteratur: David Constantine, »Outside Eden: John Clare's Descriptive Poetry«, in: J. R. Watson (Hrsg.), *An Infinite Complexity. Essays in Romanticism*, Edinburgh 1983, S. 181–201. (Nicht zu »A Spring Morning«.)

JOHN DONNE

Januar oder Februar 1572 oder 1573 London – 31.3.1631 London

John Donne, Sohn eines Kaufmanns, wurde streng katholisch erzogen. Schon im zwölften Lebensjahr wurde er in Oxford immatrikuliert, unter anderem, um dem Eid auf die Krone und die Kirche von England zu entgehen, der erst Sechzehnjährigen abverlangt wurde. Später aber trat er zur Staatskirche über. 1596 wurde er Sekretär des Lordsiegelverwalters. Durch seine heimliche Heirat mit dessen Nichte verlor er die Aussicht auf eine glanzvolle Karriere im Staatsdienst. Freunde unterstützten ihn zeitweise; der König, der auf den begabten jungen Mann aufmerksam geworden war, drängte ihn zum geistlichen Amt. Donne zögerte zunächst, widmete sich dann aber dem Studium der Theologie und wurde nach seiner Ordination Kaplan Jakobs I. und später Dekan der St. Paul's Cathedral. Er wurde einer der bedeutendsten Prediger seiner Zeit. Donnes Lyrik, größtenteils zwischen 1590 und 1611 entstanden, machte ihn zum Hauptvertreter der »metaphysical poetry«.

Text: *The Elegies and the Songs and Sonnets*, edited with an introduction and commentary by Helen Gardner, Oxford: Clarendon Press, 1965.

Sekundärliteratur: David Daiches, »A Reading of ›The Good-Morrow‹«, in Peter Amadeus Fiore (Hrsg.), *Just so Much Honor. Essays Commemorating the Four-Hundredt Anniversary of the Birth of John Donne*, University Park / London: The Pennsylvania State University Press 1972, S. 177–188; Anne Ferry, *All in War with Time*, Cambridge (Mass.) / London 1975, S. 71–78; Clay Hunt, *Donne's Poetry. Essays in Literary Analysis*, New Haven 1954, S. 52–69; Arnold Stein, *John Donne's Lyrics: the Eloquence of Action*, Minneapolis 1962, S. 65–77. (Nachdruck des Abschnittes zu »The Good-Morrow‹ in: Julian Lovelock [Hrsg.], *Donne. Songs and Sonnets. A Casebook*, London 1973, S. 156–168.)

CAROL ANN DUFFY

* 23.12.1955 Glasgow

Carol Ann Duffy verbrachte ihre Kindheit in Staffordshire und studierte in Liverpool Philosophie. Sie ist heute Professorin für Zeitgenössische Lyrik an der Manchester Metropolitan University. Schreibt auch Theaterstücke. 2009 zum ersten weiblichen »poet laureate« ernannt.

Text: *The Other Country*, London: Anvil Press Poetry, 1990. Reprinted by permission of Anvil Press Poetry, London.

Sekundärliteratur: Ruth Padel, »In otherness together«, in: *The Times Literary Supplement*, 11.–17. Mai 1990, S. 495. (Nicht zu »Hard to Say«.)

DOUGLAS DUNN

* 23.10.1942 Inchinnan (Schottland)

Douglas Dunn begann schon als Kind zu schreiben. Nach seiner Schulzeit arbeitete er als Bibliotheksassistent, ließ sich zum Bibliothekar ausbilden und arbeitete nach seiner Heirat 1964 vierzehn Monate lang in Amerika. Nach England zurückgekehrt, nahm er in Hull ein Literaturstudium auf. 1968 erhielt er eine erste Auszeichnung für seine Lyrik, 1969 erschien der Band *Terry Street*. Durch seine weitere Tätigkeit an der Universitätsbibliothek lernte er Philip Larkin, ebenfalls Bibliothekar in Hull, kennen, der Einfluß auf sein lyrisches Schaffen hatte. Neben Gedichten schreibt Dunn Radio- und Fernsehstücke, Kurzgeschichten und Literaturkritik. Nach siebzehn Jahren in England kehrte er 1984 nach Schottland zurück, das er immer als seine Heimat betrachtet hatte.

Text: *The Happier Life*, London: Faber and Faber, 1972. Reprinted by permission of Faber and Faber Ltd, London.

Sekundärliteratur: David Williams, »›They will not leave me, the lives of other people‹, The Poetry of Douglas Dunn«, in: *Studies in Scottish Literature* 23 (1988) S. 1–24. (Nicht zu »Modern Love«.)

ROBERT GRAVES

26.7.1895 London – 7.12.1985 Mallorca

Robert Ranke Graves entstammte mütterlicherseits der deutschen Adelsfamilie von Ranke, sein Urgroßvater war der Historiker Leopold von Ranke. Sein Vater war ein irischer Schulinspektor und Dichter. Robert Graves wuchs in der großbürgerlichen Atmosphäre eines viktorianischen Haushaltes auf und besuchte eine Public School. Sein Studium in Oxford wurde durch den Krieg unterbrochen. Der Krieg war eines der bedeutendsten Themen seiner frühen Lyrik, die gekennzeichnet ist durch traditionelle Formen und einen effektvollen, technisch ausgefeilten Umgang mit der Sprache. Die Begegnung (1926) und jahrelange Zusammenarbeit mit der amerikanischen Lyrikerin Laura Riding stellte einen Wendepunkt in seinem Schaffen dar. Die Transzendierung der Unmöglichkeit absoluter Liebe wurde zum dominanten Thema. »Never Such Love« entstand in dieser Zeit. In den Jahren nach ihrer Trennung (1939) schuf er seinen eigenen Mythos von der »Weißen Göttin«, der Muse, die alle wahre Dichtung inspiriert. Seit den zwanziger Jahren lebte Graves vorwiegend auf Mallorca. Neben Lyrik schrieb er auch Prosa; bekannt wurde vor allem der Roman *I, Claudius* (1934).

Text: *Collected Poems 1975,* London: Cassell, 1975. Reprinted by permission of A P Watt Ltd, London, on behalf of The Trustees of the Robert Graves Copyright Trust.

Sekundärliteratur: Michael Kirkham, *The Poetry of Robert Graves*, London 1969, S. 159.

THOM GUNN

29.8.1929 Gravesend (Kent) – 25.4.2004 San Francisco

Thom (eigtl. Thomson William) Gunn, dessen Eltern beide Journalisten waren, verbrachte eine nach eigener Aussage glückliche Kindheit in Hampstead, einem Vorort von London, war schon in jungen Jahren ein begieriger Leser und begann auch schon in dieser Zeit mit ersten Schreibversuchen. Nach zweijährigem Dienst in der Armee und einem längeren Aufenthalt in Paris studierte er in Cambridge. Die Gedichte, die in dieser Zeit entstanden, veröffentlichte er 1954 unter dem Titel *Fighting Terms*, der auf eines der Grundthemen – Liebe als Krieg – hinweist. Er zählt zu den wichtigsten Dichtern des »Movement« der fünfziger Jahre. 1954 ging er in die USA. Dort entstand auch »During an Absence«. Seine ohnehin realistische, an der Alltagswelt orientierte Sprache schien hier unter dem Einfluß der »beat generation«, eine neue Aggressivität auszudrücken, die ihm zeitweilig, und nicht ganz zu Unrecht, den Ruf der Brutalität, Amoralität, ja sogar der Neigung zum Faschismus eintrug. Seine dritte Sammlung *My Sad Captains* (1961) läßt eine Entwicklung zu kontemplativerer Lyrik erkennen. Er gilt heute als ein bedeutender philosophischer Dichter. Gunns Lyrik ist trotz ihrer bewußt zeitgenössischen Inhalte in der Form vielfach traditionell.

Text: *The Sense of Movement*, London: Faber and Faber, 1968. Reprinted by permission of Faber and Faber Ltd, London.

Sekundärliteratur: Martin Dodsworth, »Thom Gunn: Poetry as Action and Submission«, in: M. D. (Hrsg.), *The Survival of Poetry. A Contemporary Survey*, London 1970, S. 193–215. (Nicht zu »During an Absence«.)

THOMAS HARDY

2.6.1840 Higher Bockhampton (Dorset) – 11.1.1928 Max Gate bei Dorchester

Thomas Hardy veröffentlichte seinen ersten Gedichtband im Alter von achtundfünfzig Jahren und schrieb danach noch rund tausend Gedichte. Es war immer sein Wunsch gewesen, Dichter zu werden, doch verschiedene Umstände hatten ihn zunächst zu anderen Tätigkeiten veranlaßt. Er wuchs in dörflicher Umgebung auf. Sein Vater war ein Steinmetz, der sonntags in der Kirche die Violine spielte, seine Mutter eine ernsthafte und arbeitsame Frau, die wollte, daß ihr Sohn es zu etwas brächte. Das Gedicht »A Church Romance« nimmt auf die Brautzeit seiner Eltern Bezug. Thomas wurde auf die Schule nach Dorchester geschickt und war dann Lehrling bei einem Architekten. Seine Freizeit verbrachte er mit eigenen Studien, so daß er, obwohl er keine Universität besuchte, ein außerordentlich gebildeter Mensch war. Gleichzeitig nahm er aktiven Anteil am bäuerlichen Leben seiner Heimat. 1874 gab er seinen Beruf als Architekt auf und widmete sich dem Schreiben. Er wurde berühmt als Romancier, der den Kampf des Menschen gegen ein unerbittliches, aber gleichgültiges Schicksal zu seinem Thema machte. Sein unermüdliches Schreiben und Revidieren widerspricht seiner eigenen Behauptung, daß seine Romane vor allem Broterwerb gewesen seien. In seinem späteren Leben aber wandte er sich fast ausschließlich der Lyrik zu. Sein Pessimismus angesichts der Ironie des menschlichen Lebens, der ihm trotz seines Erfolges auch bezüglich seines eigenen Lebens nicht fremd war, und seine Liebe zur Natur prägen seine Gedichte wie schon zuvor seine Romane.

Text: *The Variorum Edition of the Complete Poems of Thomas Hardy*, edited by James Gibson, London: Macmillan, 1978.

Sekundärliteratur: Howard Baker, »Hardy's Poetic Certitude«, in: *Southern Review* 6 (1940/41) S. 49–63. (Nachdruck in: James Gibson / Trevor Johnson [Hrsg.], *Thomas Hardy: Poems. A Casebook*, London 1979, S. 137–146); Rosemary L. Eakins, »The Mellstock Quire and Tess in Hardy's Poetry«, in: Patricia Clements / Juliet Grindle, *The Poetry of Thomas Hardy*, London 1980, S. 52–68.

SEAMUS HEANEY

* 13.4.1939 Mossbawm bei Castledawson (Nordirland)

Seamus Heaney wuchs als ältestes von neun Kindern eines katholischen Bauern auf, besuchte die örtliche Grundschule und erhielt Stipendien für die höhere Schule in Londonderry sowie die Universität in Belfast, an der er später auch selbst lehrte. Er veröffentlichte seine ersten Gedichte in Zeitschriften, zunächst in Belfast, dann auch in London, arbeitete zeitweilig als Lehrer und begründete seinen Ruf als einer der bedeutendsten zeitgenössischen Dichter mit dem Band *Death of a Naturalist*, der 1966 erschien, ein Jahr nach seiner Heirat mit Marie Devlin, der das darin enthaltene »Poem« gewidmet ist. Nach einer Gastdozentur in Kalifornien siedelte er in die Republik Irland über und hat dort neben seiner freiberuflichen Tätigkeit einen Lehrauftrag an einem College inne. Seine Gedichte spiegeln seine komplexe kulturelle Identität als Brite wie auch als Mitglied der katholischen Minderheit in Nordirland, die durch ihre Affinität zur Republik Irland gekennzeichet ist, und weisen Einflüsse irischer wie auch englischer Dichtungstradition auf. 1995 Nobelpreis für Literatur.

Text: *Death of a Naturalist*, London: Faber and Faber, 1969. Reprinted by permission of Faber and Faber Ltd, London.

Sekundärliteratur: John Wilson Foster, »The Poetry of Seamus Heaney«, in: *Critical Quarterly* 16 (1974) S. 35–48. (Nicht zu »Poem for Marie«.)

ALFRED EDWARD HOUSMAN

26.3.1859 Fockbury (Worcestershire) – 30.4.1936 Cambridge

Alfred Edward Housman, Sohn eines Rechtsanwalts, studierte in Oxford klassische Philologie und arbeitete anschließend zehn Jahre lang im Patentamt in London. Seine zahlreichen Veröffentlichungen zu Autoren der griechischen und römischen Antike erwarben ihm eine Lateinprofessur in London, später in Cambridge. Zur Verwunderung seiner Freunde und Bekannten veröffentlichte er 1896 *A Shropshire Lad*, eine Sammlung von Gedichten, die im ländlichen Milieu angesiedelt sind und vielfach balladenhafte Züge tragen, aufgrund ihres Pessimismus und ihrer klassischen Schlichtheit der Form aber kaum als volkstümlich gelten können. Zwei weitere Bände folgten, der letzte postum.

Text: *The Collected Poems of A. E. Housman*, London: Jonathan Cape, 1952.

Sekundärliteratur: Edward W. Rosenheim Jr., *What Happens in Literature. A Guide to Poetry, Drama, and Fiction*, Chicago/London 1960, S. 5–13.

TED HUGHES

17.8.1930 Mytholmroyd (Yorkshire) – 28.10.1998 London

Ted (Edward James) Hughes verbrachte seine frühe Kindheit in der Moorlandschaft Yorkshires, die er als düster und gleichzeitig erhaben empfand und deren Atmosphäre ihren Niederschlag in seinen Gedichten hatte. Bereits in seiner Schulzeit wurde sein Interesse an Lyrik geweckt, er begann als Fünfzehnjähriger selbst zu schreiben. Nach seinem Militärdienst studierte er in Cambridge zunächst englische Literatur, dann Archäologie und Anthropologie. 1956 begegnete er der amerikanischen Lyrikerin Sylvia Plath, die er im selben Jahr heiratete. Auf ihre Anregung hin nahm er an einem Lyrikwettbewerb teil, den er gewann, woraufhin seine erste Sammlung *The Hawk in the Rain* (1957) in Amerika und England veröffentlicht wurde. »September« gehört zu diesen Gedichten. Nach zwei Jahren wenig befriedigender Lehrtätigkeit an einem amerikanischen College kehrten Ted Hughes und seine Frau nach England zurück. Ihre Ehe war außerordentlich anregend für beider schriftstellerische Arbeit, persönliche Spannungen führten jedoch zur Trennung. Nach dem Freitod Sylvia Plaths (1963) widmete Hughes sich in den darauffolgenden Jahren intensiver der Herausgabe der Werke seiner Frau als seiner eigenen schriftstellerischen Arbeit, bis er 1967 wieder mit einem eigenen Gedichtband, dem mehrere weitere folgten, an die Öffentlichkeit trat. Hughes' Lyrik ist geprägt vom Thema des der Natur entfremdeten Menschen, dessen Instinkte durch seine Rationalität und gesellschaftliche Konventionen unterdrückt sind, Tiere gehören zu seinen wesentlichen Symbolgestalten. Hughes' Interesse am Okkulten und Mythologischen bestimmte wesentlich seine Schaffensphase der späten sechziger Jahre. In späteren Gedichten knüpft er wieder stärker an die konkrete Erfahrungswelt an. Neben seiner dichterischen Arbeit begann er sich mit Landwirtschaft zu befassen. 1984 wurde Hughes zum »poet laureate« ernannt.

Text: *The Hawk in the Rain*, London: Faber and Faber, 1968. Reprinted by permission of Faber and Faber Ltd, London.

Sekundärliteratur: Keith Sagar, *The Art of Ted Hughes,* Cambridge 1975. (Nicht zu »September«.)

ELIZABETH JENNINGS

18.7.1926 Boston (Lincolnshire) – 25.10.2001 Oxford

Elizabeth Jennings entdeckte die Lyrik im Alter von dreizehn Jahren. Sie las Keats und Coleridge und begann eigene Verse zu schreiben, später wurde ihr T. S. Eliot wichtig und dann ganz entscheidend Edwin Muir und Robert Frost. Ihre Jugend stand unter dem Einfluß des Krieges. Sie studierte später in Oxford und zählte von Anfang an zu den Dichtern des »Movement«, obwohl sie selbst darin nie eine feste Gruppe sah, sondern individuelle Dichter, deren Werke Parallelen aufweisen, die in der Zeit selbst begründet sind. Ohnehin nimmt sie eine Sonderstellung innerhalb des »Movement« ein als einzige Frau und gläubige Katholikin sowie aufgrund ihrer beruflichen Tätigkeit als Bibliothekarin und Verlagslektorin, durch die sie sich vom akademischen Betrieb löste. Ihre Lyrik ist von schlichter Klarheit in Gedanklichkeit und Form, sie wirkt kühl und beherrscht, nachdenklich und unideologisch, dennoch persönlich und unmittelbar.

Text: *Collected Poems 1953–1985*, Manchester: Carcanet Press, 1986. Reprinted by permission of David Higham Associates Ltd, London.

Sekundärliteratur: Margaret Byers, »Cautious Vision: Recent British Poetry by Women«, in: Michael Schmidt / Grevel Lindop (Hrsg.), *British Poetry since 1960. A Critical Survey*, Oxford 1972, S. 74–84. (Nicht zu »Winter Love«.)

JOHN KEATS

29. oder 31.10.1795 London – 23.2.1821 Rom

John Keats war der Sohn eines Mietstallverwalters. Nach dem frühen Tod seiner Eltern begann er eine Lehre bei einem Wundarzt und arbeitete kurze Zeit in einem Londoner Krankenhaus. Er glaubte sich aber selbst für diesen Beruf ungeeignet und beschloß 1816, unter anderem auf den Rat Shelleys hin, sich seiner eigentlichen Neigung, der Dichtung, zu widmen. Er hatte bereits intensive literarische Studien betrieben und auch eigene Gedichte in einer Zeitschrift veröffentlicht. Von besonderem Einfluß waren für ihn die elisabethanische Lyrik und die antike Mythologie. Sein erster Gedichtband, der sich deutlich von den poetischen Konventionen des 18. Jahrhunderts absetzte, zeigte vielversprechendes Talent, erhielt aber auch, ebenso wie das lange allegorische Gedicht *Endymion*, harsche Kritik. 1817 begegnete Keats Fanny Brawne, einem jungen, etwas oberflächlichen Mädchen, das seine Leidenschaft kaum zu erwidern vermochte. Keats' lyrisches Schaffen erreichte seinen Höhepunkt in den Jahren 1818/19, in denen er unter anderem seine bedeutenden Oden schrieb. Eine sich rapide verschlimmernde Tuberkulose veranlaßte ihn zu einer Reise nach Italien. Auf dem Weg dorthin schrieb er sein letztes Gedicht, das Sonett »Bright star! would I were steadfast as thou art«.

Text: *The Poetical Works of John Keats*, edited by H. W. Garrod, Oxford: Clarendon Press, 1958.

Sekundärliteratur: David Ormerod, »Nature's Eremite: Keats and the Liturgy of Passion«, in: *Keats-Shelley Journal* 16 (Winter 1967) S. 73–77; M. L. Rosenthal, *Poetry and the Common Life*, New York 1974, S. 123–125.

PHILIP LARKIN

9.8.1922 Coventry – 2.12.1985 Hull

Philip Larkin galt jahrelang als Englands inoffizieller »poet laureate«, als der Dichter, der wie kaum ein anderer in seiner Lyrik englische Nachkriegswirklichkeit dargestellt und verarbeitet hat. Seine Kindheit bezeichnete er später als normal, wenn auch nicht besonders glücklich, da er unter seiner Schüchternheit, seinem Stottern und seiner Kurzsichtigkeit litt. Sein Studium in Oxford, wo er mit Schriftstellern wie Kingsley Amis und John Wain Freundschaft schloß, war eine für seine Persönlichkeitsentwicklung bedeutende Phase, die gefolgt wurde von einer Zeit außerordentlicher Kreativität, in der er die *North Ship*-Gedichte (1945) und zwei Romane schrieb (*Jill*, 1946; *Girl in Winter*, 1947). Er arbeitete als Bibliothekar zunächst in Wellington, dann in Leicester, Belfast und Hull. Die Belfaster Zeit ist durch eine zweite sehr produktive Phase gekennzeichnet. Hier entdeckte er Thomas Hardys Gedichte, die ihn lehrten, das Alltägliche und Offensichtliche nicht zu fürchten, sondern zur Grundlage seiner Dichtung zu machen. Sein wohl wichtigstes Werk *The Whitsun Weddings* (1964) stellt eine konsequente Weiterentwicklung seines eigenen Stils dar, der geprägt ist von Realismus, Ironie und Humor, wo jedes Gedicht seine eigene konkrete Fiktionalität besitzt wie ein Roman in nuce. Die Begrenztheit und Isolation der menschlichen Existenz ist sein wiederkehrendes Thema. Neben seinen eigenen Arbeiten gab er *The Oxford Book of Twentieth Century English Verse* (1973) heraus. Nach seinem letzten Gedichtband *High Windows* (1974) beschloß Larkin, keine Gedichte mehr zu schreiben.

Text: *The Whitsun Weddings*, London: Faber and Faber, [5]1970. Reprinted by permission of Faber and Faber Ltd, London.

Sekundärliteratur: George Sutherland Fraser, *Essays on Twentieth-Century Poets*, Leicester: Leicester University Press 1977, S. 248 f.; Hermann Peschmann, »Philip Larkin: Laureate of the Common Man«, in: *English* 24 (1975) S. 49–58; John Woolley, »Larkin: Romance, Fiction and Myth«, in: *English* 35 (1968) S. 237–267.

DAVID HERBERT LAWRENCE

11.9.1885 Eastwood – 2.3.1930 Vence (Südfrankreich)

David Herbert Lawrence war der Sohn eines Bergmannes und einer Lehrerin und wuchs in beschränkten Verhältnissen auf, was ihn jedoch nicht daran hinderte, seine intellektuellen Neigungen schon früh zu entwickeln. Er erhielt ein Stipendium für die Nottingham High School, absolvierte anschließend eine Lehrerausbildung und arbeitete drei Jahre lang an einer Londoner Schule.

Während dieser Zeit erschienen seine ersten Gedichte in Zeitschriften und er veröffentlichte seinen ersten Roman *The White Peacock* (1911). Im April 1912 lernte er Frieda Weekley geb. von Richthofen kennen, die seine Lebensgefährtin und spätere Ehefrau wurde. Die Beziehung bewirkte in Lawrence eine Befreiung von den Denkmustern und Konventionen seines bisherigen Lebens, die sich äußerlich in einer neuen, unsteten Lebensweise zeigte, welche das Paar in die verschiedensten Länder (vornehmlich Italien und Mexiko) führte, die ihren Niederschlag aber auch in Lawrences Dichtung fand, in der Abkehr von traditionellen Reimformen und der Zuwendung zum reimlosen Vers und freien Rhythmus (u. a. *Birds Beasts and Flowers*, 1923; *Pansies*, 1929). »Andraitx – Pomegranate Flowers« entstand vermutlich 1929 auf einer Mallorcareise. Erschüttert von den Kriegsereignissen bekämpfte Lawrence die Lebensfeindlichkeit der menschlichen Gesellschaft und fand einen Gegenentwurf in der elementaren Lebenskraft der Natur, in der Mythologie und in primitiven Kulturen.

Text: *The Complete Poems of D. H. Lawrence*, Vol. 2, collected and edited with an introduction and notes by Vivian de Sola Pinto and Warren Roberts, London: Heinemann, 1972.

Sekundärliteratur: M. J. Lockwood, *A Study of the Poems of D. H. Lawrence. Thinking in Poetry*, London/Basingstoke 1987. (Nicht zu »Andraitx – Pomegranate Flowers«.)

ROGER McGOUGH

* 9.11.1937 Liverpool

Die Karriere Roger McGoughs hat manchen Bezugspunkt zu der der Beatles, die etwa zur gleichen Zeit von seiner Heimatstadt Liverpool aus die Musikszene veränderten. Er gilt als »pop poet«, dessen Lyrik vor allem im öffentlichen Vortrag lebt und ein, zumeist jüngeres, Massenpublikum erreicht. McGough stammte aus einer »working-class«-Familie, sein Vater war Dockarbeiter, und er schloß sich Mitte der sechziger Jahre der Popmusikgruppe »The Scaffold« an, die durch satirische Texte ihre Kritik am Establishment zum Ausdruck brachte. Er besaß jedoch zu dieser Zeit bereits ein Lehrerdiplom und hatte an zwei Liverpooler Schulen unterrichtet – eine Erfahrung, die er besonders in seinem Lyrikband *in the glassroom* verarbeitete. Neben Gedichten schrieb

McGough auch Bücher für Kinder. Er arbeitet zudem für Theater, Radio und Fernsehen. McGough zählt neben Brian Patten und Adrian Henri zu den »Liverpool poets«, die von Einfluß auf die englische »underground poetry« waren und sind.

Text: *Selected Poems 1967–1987*, London: Jonathan Cape, 1989. Reprinted by permission of Random Century Group, London.

Sekundärliteratur: Grevel Lindop, »Poetry, Rhetoric and the Mass Audience: The Case of the Liverpool Poets«, in: Michael Schmidt / Grevel Lindop (Hrsg.), *British Poetry Since 1960. A Critical Survey*, Oxford 1972, S. 92–106.

ANDREW MARVELL

31.3.1621 Winestead (Yorkshire) – 18.8.1678 London

Marvells Leben stand unter dem Einfluß politischer Umbrüche – dem Sturz der Stuarts, der Errichtung des Commonwealth unter Cromwell und der Restauration des Königshauses. Er studierte in Cambridge und bereiste dann einige Jahre den Kontinent. Zu dieser Zeit sympathisierte er noch mit den Royalisten. 1657 jedoch wurde er Miltons Mitarbeiter im Staatsrat und inoffizieller »Hofdichter« Cromwells. Nach Cromwells Tod unterstützte er die Politik von dessen Sohn als Parlamentsabgeordneter für Hull. Nach der Restauration behielt er dieses Amt bei, verbrachte aber längere Zeit im Ausland und schrieb bissige Satiren gegen die Korruption des Parlaments sowie die religiöse Intoleranz der Regierung. Zu Lebzeiten basierte Marvells literarischer Ruhm vorwiegend auf seinen Streitschriften und Satiren. Seine lyrischen Gedichte, meist vor der Restauration entstanden und in der Tradition Donnes stehend, wurden, ebenso wie die meisten seiner politischen Gedichte, erst nach seinem Tod gedruckt. Ihre eigentliche Wertschätzung setzte im 20. Jahrhundert ein.

Text: *The Poems and Letters of Andrew Marvell*, edited by H. M. Margoliouth, Oxford: Clarendon Press, 1952.

Sekundärliteratur: Jules Brody, »The Resurrection of the Body: A New Reading of Marvell's ›To His Coy Mistress‹«, in: *Journal of English Literary History* 56 (1989) S. 53–79; Wolfgang Iser, »Andrew Marvell (1621–1678): ›To his Coy Mistress‹«, in: *Die Neueren Sprachen* 12 (1957) S. 555–577; Reinhold Schiffer,

»Andrew Marvell, ›To His Coy Mistress‹«, in: Reinhold Schiffer / Hermann J. Weiand (Hrsg.), *Insight III. Analyses of English and American Poetry*, Frankfurt 1972, S. 188–196.

GEORGE MEREDITH

12.2.1828 Portsmouth – 18.5.1909 Dorking (Surrey)

George Meredith, Sohn eines Schneiders, verbrachte seine Kindheit in Portsmouth, unterbrochen von einem zweijährigen Aufenthalt in Neuwied am Rhein, wo er eine Schule der Herrnhuter besuchte. Anschließend ging er bei einem Anwalt in die Lehre. 1851 veröffentlichte er auf eigene Kosten einen ersten Gedichtband, 1862 folgte ein zweiter, *Modern Love*, der autobiographischen Bezug zu seiner Ehe mit Mary Ellen Nicholls, der Tochter des Dichters Peacock, hat, die ihn 1858 verließ. In fünfzig sonettähnlichen Gedichten behandelt er darin die Geschichte einer von Spannungen und Versöhnungsversuchen gezeichneten Ehe. Diese desillusionierende Behandlung des Themas Liebe steht in deutlichem Gegensatz zu den idealisierenden Sonettsequenzen der Renaissance. Die folgenden Jahre, in denen Meredith fast nur Romane schrieb, begründeten seinen Ruf als einer der letzten großen viktorianischen Romanciers. Gleichzeitig arbeitete er als Lektor für den Verlag Chapman and Hall. In den achtziger Jahren veröffentlichte er weitere Gedichtbände. Er wandte sich zunehmend auch politischen Themen wie der Französischen Revolution und den Napoleonischen Kriegen zu.

Text: *Poems*, Vol. 1, New York: Russell & Russell, 1968.

Sekundärliteratur: Hans Ostrom, »The Disappearance of Tragedy in Meredith's *Modern Love*«, in: *Victorian Newsletter* 63 (Frühjahr 1983) S. 26–30; Arthur L. Simpson Jr., »Meredith's Pessimistic Humanism: A New Reading of *Modern Love*«, in: *Modern Philology* 67 (1970) S. 341–356; Cynthia Grant Tucker, »Meredith's Broken Laurel: *Modern Love* and the Renaissance Sonnet Tradition«, in: *Victorian Poetry* 10 (1972) S. 351–365.

CHARLOTTE MEW

15.11.1869 London – 24.3.1928 London

Charlotte Mew, eine Enkelin des bekannten Architekten Henry Kendall, wuchs unter bedrückenden familiären Umständen auf. Drei ihrer Brüder starben während ihrer Kindheit, zwei weitere Geschwister mußten wegen psychischer Störungen in eine Heilanstalt eingewiesen werden. Charlotte wurde privat unterrichtet und besuchte später das University College. Sie war ein lebhaftes, oft etwas rebellisches Kind und auch als Erwachsene unausgeglichen in ihrem Verhalten – extravagant, doch von Spannungen gequält und auf der Suche nach einem inneren Halt. Sie schrieb Gedichte, Kurzgeschichten und Essays, die in Zeitschriften veröffentlicht wurden. Ihr erster Gedichtband *The Farmer's Bride* brachte ihr breitere Anerkennung unter anderem von Virginia Woolf und Thomas Hardy, der in ihr die beste Lyrikerin ihrer Zeit sah. Der Tod ihrer Schwester Anne, mit der sie zusammen gelebt hatte, war ein schwerer Schlag für sie. Ein Jahr darauf nahm sie sich das Leben.

Text: *Collected Poems and Prose*, edited by Val Warner, London: Virago Press, 1982.

Sekundärliteratur: Michael Schmidt, *An Introduction to Fifty Modern British Poets*, London/Sydney 1979, S. 57–63. (Nicht zu »I so Liked Spring«.)

SYLVIA PLATH

27.10.1932 Boston – 11.2.1963 London

Sylvia Plath gehört nur bedingt in die Reihe englischer Lyriker, denn sie stammt aus den USA und lebte dort, bis sie im Rahmen eines Fulbright-Stipendiums 1955 nach Cambridge kam. In England entstanden jedoch ihre bedeutendsten Gedichte. Sylvia Plath entstammte einer deutsch-österreichischen Familie. Sie verlor ihren Vater, einen Dozenten der Naturwissenschaften, mit acht Jahren, eine Erfahrung, die sie nachhaltig beeinflußte. Sie war eine außergewöhnlich begabte Studentin und gewann bei einem Wettbewerb einer Zeitschrift mit einem ihrer Gedichte einen vierwöchigen New-York-Aufenthalt als Gastredakteurin. Dieser Lebensabschnitt war aber auch begleitet von tiefen Depressionen, die zu einem Selbstmordversuch und psychiatrischer Behandlung führten. Ihr Roman *The Bell Jar* (1963) verarbeitet diese Erlebnisse. In Cambridge lernte sie Ted Hughes kennen, den sie 1956 heiratete. Nach zweijähriger Lehrtätigkeit in Amerika beschloß das Paar, in England zu leben. Die folgenden Jahre waren von außerordentlicher Kreativität und Produktivität. Ende 1962 trennte sich Sylvia Plath von Ted Hughes, ging nach London und setzte dort in neuerlicher Depression Anfang 1963 ihrem Leben ein Ende. Krankheit, Schmerz, Wahnsinn und vor allem Tod gehören zu den wiederkehrenden Themen in Sylvia Plaths Lyrik. Autobiographisch motiviert, werden sie zu Metaphern des menschlichen Seins, das bestimmt ist durch Einsamkeit, Fremdbestimmtheit, Leid und Angst und das Ringen um schöpferische Kraft, Fruchtbarkeit, Liebe, Lebenshoffnung, die ihren Ausdruck finden im natürlich-organischen Lebensprozeß wie auch in dichterischer Produktivität. Insofern kreisen ihre Gedichte auch um ihre Rolle als Frau und als Dichterin, um ihre eigene Todesangst und Todessehnsucht, wären aber als Bekenntnislyrik zu einseitig gedeutet.

Text: *Collected Poems*, edited by Ted Hughes, London: Faber and Faber, 1981. Reprinted by permission of Faber and Faber Ltd, London.

Sekundärliteratur: Margaret Dickie Uroff, »Sylvia Plath's Women«, in: *Concerning Poetry* 7 (1974) S. 50 f.

CHRISTINA ROSSETTI

5.12.1830 London – 29.12.1894 London

Christina Georgina Rossetti war eine Tochter des italienischen Dichters und Konservators Gabriele Rossetti, der nach der Revolution von 1820 nach England kam und dort Professor für Italienisch wurde. Wie ihre drei Geschwister genoß sie die Vorteile eines der Kunst zugewandten Elternhauses. Schon früh begann sie selbst sowohl in italienischer als auch englischer Sprache Gedichte zu schreiben. Krankheit und Tod des Vaters machten es notwendig, daß sie ihrer Mutter als Hilfslehrerin an einer Tagesschule assistierte, mehr noch aber entsprach es ihrer tiefreligiösen Natur, sich kirchlichen und karitativen Aufgaben zu widmen. Sie löste eine Verlobung mit dem Maler James Collinson, da dieser sich nach vorübergehender Sympathie für die anglikanische Kirche wieder dem römischen Katholizismus zuwandte, litt aber unter der Erfahrung der Entsagung. Ihre Liebeslyrik wie ihre Gedichte überhaupt sind geprägt von einem melancholischen Ton und religiöser Gedanklichkeit, wie die Sonettsequenz *Monna Innominata* zeigt. Ihre späteren Werke sind vielfach von sehr erbaulichem Charakter und wirken heute eher veraltet.

Text: *The Complete Poems of Christina Rossetti*, Vol. 2, edited, with textual notes and introductions, by R. W. Crump, Baton Rouge / London: Louisiana State University Press, 1986.

Sekundärliteratur: William Whitla, »Questioning the Convention. Christina Rossetti's Sonnet Sequence *Monna Innominata*«, in: David A. Kent (Hrsg.), *The Achievement of Christina Rossetti*, Ithaca/London 1987, S. 82–131.

DANTE GABRIEL ROSSETTI

12.5.1828 London – 9.4.1882 Birchington-on-Sea (Kent)

Dante Gabriel Rossettis künstlerisches Talent lag sowohl im Bereich der Dichtung als auch der Malerei. Beides wurde von Jugend an – er war der Sohn des italienischen Dichters und Konservators Gabriele Rossetti – gefördert. Als Dreizehnjähriger besuchte er eine Zeichenschule, fünf Jahre später wurde er in die Royal Academy aufgenommen. Gleichzeitig begann er mit einer Übersetzung der Werke Dantes und seiner Zeitgenossen und schrieb eigene Sonette. Er war Mitbegründer der Präraffaeliten, einer Gruppe von Künstlern, die den Klassizismus des 19. Jahrhunderts ablehnten und sich einem am Mittelalter orientierten symbolisierenden Ästhetizismus zuwandten. Rossettis produktivste Phase lag in den Jahren 1850–60. Der Tod seiner Frau, die 1862 nach nur zwei Ehejahren starb, veranlaßte ihn, seine Manuskripte mit ihr zu begraben. Er erlangte sie später wieder, doch das Leben des Dichters vollzog sich mehr und mehr unter dem Einfluß von Chloral, mit dem er neuralgische Schmerzen und Schlaflosigkeit zu bekämpfen suchte. Es gelang ihm noch einmal, seine dichterische Kraft zu aktivieren – in dieser Zeit entstand der Zyklus *The House of Life* –, doch seine physische Kondition ließ keinen Neubeginn mehr zu.

Text: *The Works of Dante Gabriel Rossetti*, edited with preface and notes by William M. Rossetti, London: Ellis, 1911.

Sekundärliteratur: Joan Rees, *The Poetry of Dante Gabriel Rossetti: Modes of Self-Expression*, Cambridge 1981, S. 160–166; David G. Riede, *Dante Gabriel Rossetti and the Limits of Victorian Vision*, Ithaca/London 1983, S. 152 f.

WILLIAM SHAKESPEARE

23.(?)4.1564 Stratford-upon-Avon – 23.4.1616 Stratford-upon-Avon

William Shakespeare war das dritte Kind und der älteste Sohn des Händlers und Handschuhmachers John Shakespeare, der eine angesehene Position in der Stadt besaß, aber zunehmend in finanzielle Schwierigkeiten geriet. William besuchte die Lateinschule in Stratford, heiratete 1582 Ann Hathaway und zog schon bald nach der Geburt von drei Kindern allein nach London, wo er sich dem Theater zuwandte. Als Schauspieler, Stückeschreiber und Teilhaber gehörte er der Truppe »The Lord Chamberlain's Men« an, die auch bei Hof auftrat. In den ersten Londoner Jahren verfaßte er hundertvierundfünfzig Sonette, die zum Teil an einen jungen Mann von Adel gerichtet sind. Ob ein autobiographischer Bezug vorliegt – es könnte sich um den als Mäzen bekannten Earl of Southampton oder um William Herbert of Pembroke handeln – konnte nicht geklärt werden. Die letzten Jahre seines Lebens verbrachte Shakespeare wiederum in Stratford.

Text: *Shakespeare's Sonnets*, edited with analytic commentary by Stephen Booth, New Haven / London: Yale University Press, 1978.

Sekundärliteratur: Stephen Booth (Hrsg.), *Shakespeare's Sonnets*, New Haven / London: Yale University Press, 1978, S. 384–392. (Nachdruck in: Harold Bloom [Hrsg.], *Shakespeare's Sonnets. Modern Critical Interpretations*, New York / New Haven / Philadelphia 1987, S. 47–54.); Hilton Landry, »The Marriage of True Minds. Truth and Error in Sonnet 116«, in: *Shakespeare Studies* 3 (1967) S. 98–110; Robert Levine, »The Magnanimity of True Love. Shakespeare's Sonnet 116«, in: *Essays in Arts and Sciences* 16 (Mai 1987) S. 1–8; Theodor Wolpers, »William Shakespeare. Sonnets XVIII, XXIX, XXX, LX, LXXIII, CXVI, CXXIX, CXXXXVI«, in: Karl Heinz Göller (Hrsg.), *Die englische Lyrik I. Von der Renaissance bis zur Gegenwart*, Düsseldorf 1968, S. 76–133.

(SIR) PHILIP SIDNEY

30.11.1554 Penshurst (Kent) – 17.10.1586 Arnheim

Sir Philip Sidney, aus adliger Familie stammend, war ein äußerst begabter Schüler und Student. Nachdem er Oxford wegen der dort herrschenden Pest verlassen hatte, bereiste er den Kontinent, wo er sich an Fürsten- und Königshöfen aufhielt und seine Studien auf den verschiedensten Gebieten fortsetzte. Er verliebte sich in die Tochter des Grafen von Essex, die er in seinem Sonettzyklus *Astrophel and Stella* besang. Im Dienst der Königin Elisabeth I. versah er vielfältige diplomatische Aufgaben und unterstützte den europäischen Protestantismus. Als Gouverneur von Flushing (Niederlande) nahm er am Krieg gegen die Spanier teil und starb an den Folgen einer Verwundung. Sein literarischer Ruhm beruht neben den Sonetten und seinem Roman *Arcadia* auf der theoretischen Schrift *An Apology for Poetry* (1595).

Text: *The Poems of Sir Philip Sidney*, edited by William A. Ringler Jr., Oxford: Clarendon Press, 1962.

Sekundärliteratur: Richard B. Young, »English Petrarke: A Study of Sidney's *Astrophel and Stella«*, in: Richard B. Young / W. Todd Furniss / William G. Madsen, *Three Studies in the Renaissance: Sidney, Jonson, Milton*, New Haven: Yale University Press, 1958, S. 1–8.

WILLIAM WORDSWORTH

7.4.1770 Cockermouth (Cumberland) – 23.4.1850 Rydal Mount bei Grasmere (Cumberland)

William Wordsworth war früh verwaist, durch das Bemühen seiner Vormünder konnte er jedoch eine Grammar School und ab 1787 das St. John's College in Cambridge besuchen. Er fand wenig Gefallen am akademischen Betrieb und verbrachte einen großen Teil seiner Zeit mit ausgedehnten Spaziergängen, sportlicher Betätigung und im gesellschaftlichen Umgang mit Kommilitonen. 1790 und 1792 bereiste er Frankreich und begeisterte sich für die Ziele der Französischen Revolution. Unentschlossen hinsichtlich seiner Berufswahl, wollte er auch genügend Französisch lernen, um sich für eine Hauslehrerstelle zu qualifizieren. Er veröffentlichte erste Gedichte, noch weitgehend in der Tradition Popes stehend. Eine kleine Erbschaft ermöglichte es ihm 1795, sich zusammen mit seiner Schwester Dorothy als freischaffender Dichter in Somerset niederzulassen. Er war befreundet mit Southey und vor allem mit Coleridge, mit dem zusammen er 1798 die *Lyrical Ballads* veröffentlichte, die als der Beginn der englischen Romantik betrachtet werden. Während eines längeren Deutschlandaufenthaltes entstanden die »Lucy-Poems«, deren Hauptfigur wohl keinen realen Bezug hat. 1802 heiratete Wordsworth Mary Hutchinson. Er lebte, von längeren Reisen abgesehen, weitgehend zurückgezogen, trotzdem galt er als eine der bedeutendsten Persönlichkeiten des literarischen Lebens und wurde 1843 »poet laureate«. Er hatte inzwischen die revolutionären Ideen seiner Jugend aufgegeben und war zu einem konservativen Patrioten geworden.

Text: *The Poetical Works of William Wordsworth*, Vol. 2, edited from the manuscripts with textual and critical notes by E. de Selincourt, Oxford: Clarendon Press, 1944.

Sekundärliteratur: William P. Dawson, »The Perceptual Bond in ›Strange Fits of Passion‹«, in: *The Wordsworth Circle* 13 (1982) S. 96 f.; Frances C. Ferguson, »The Lucy Poems: Wordsworth's Quest for a Poetic Object«, in: *English Literary History* 40 (1973) S. 532–548; Spencer Hall, »Wordsworth's ›Lucy‹ Poems: Context and Meaning«, in: *Studies in Romanticism* 10 (1971) S. 159–175; Virginia Ireys, »The Death of the Muse: Wordsworth's Lucy as Pastoral Heroine«, in: *Papers on Language and Literature* 24 (1988) S. 384–403; J. R. Watson, »Lucy and the Earth-Mother«, in: *Essays in Criticism* 27 (1977) S. 187–202; John Price, »Wordsworth's Lucy«, in: *American Imago* 31 (1974) S. 360–377.

WILLIAM BUTLER YEATS

13.6.1865 Dublin – 28.1.1939 Roquebrune bei Nizza

William Butler Yeats war der Sohn des Malers John Butler Yeats, der den Präraffaeliten nahestand. Als kleines Kind schon zog er mit seiner Familie nach London, blieb jedoch Irland durch häufige Besuche verbunden. Seine Schulbildung war nur mäßig, zumal er ein unaufmerksamer Schüler war. Erst allmählich gewann er Neigung zur Literatur, nachdem er zunächst stärker naturwissenschaftlich interessiert gewesen war. Er studierte an der Dublin School of Art, besaß jedoch kein herausragendes Talent für bildende Kunst.

Gleichzeitig entwickelte er einen starken Hang zum Okkultismus; er war Mitbegründer der Dublin Hermetic Society, wurde Mitglied der Theosophischen Gesellschaft in London und schließlich des Rosenkreuzer-Ordens. Sein Interesse an der nationalen Identität Irlands verstärkte sich unter dem Einfluß Maud Gonnes, einer radikalen Republikanerin, in die er sich 1889 verliebte, die ihn aber nicht heiraten wollte. Ihr ist vermutlich das Gedicht »The Rose of the World« gewidmet. Mehr noch als die politische Frage bewegte ihn die Förderung der irischen Kultur. Er begründete 1904 das Abbey Theatre in Dublin als irisches Nationaltheater, für das er selbst Versdramen schrieb, und befaßte sich intensiv mit irischer Volkstradition und keltischer Mythologie. Yeats' erste Gedichte wurden 1885 veröffentlicht, 1908 erschien eine achtbändige Ausgabe *Collected Works*. Yeats war zu diesem Zeitpunkt ein anerkannter Lyriker und Dramatiker. Seine besten und reifsten Gedichte wurden jedoch erst danach geschrieben (*The Wild Swans at Coole*, 1919; *The Tower*, 1928; *The Winding Stair and Other Poems*, 1933), als er sich von seinen Vorbildern und zeitgenössischen Strömungen soweit gelöst hatte, daß er seinen eigenen Stil und sein eigenes Weltbild entwickeln konnte, das Anregungen aus der neuplatonischen Philosophie, aus der Theologie, aus der östlichen, jüdischen und christlichen Mystik und der keltischen Mythologie verarbeitete. Yeats erhielt 1923 den Literaturnobelpreis. Seine nationalistischen Hoffnungen erfüllten sich, zumindest teilweise, mit der Gründung des Irischen Freistaates, dessen Senator er zeitweilig war.

Text: *The Poems. A New Edition*, edited by Richard J. Finneran, London: Macmillan, 1984.

Sekundärliteratur: Hiram Haydn, »The Last of the Romantics: An Introduction to the Symbolism of William Butler Yeats«, in: *Sewanee Review* 55 (1947) S. 297–323. (Allgemein zum Bild der Rose bei Yeats.); Gloria Kline, *The Last Courtly Lover. Yeats and the Idea of Woman*, Ann Arbor (Mich.) 1976, S. 11 f.; W. Y. Tindall, »The Symbolism of W. B. Yeats«, in: John Unterecker (Hrsg.), *Yeats. A Collection of Critical Essays*, Englewood Cliffs (N. J.): Prentice-Hall, 1963, S. 43–53.

Inhalt